ASK THE CHILDREN

Experiences of physical disability in the school years

Nicola Madge and Meg Fassam

BATSFORD ACADEMIC AND EDUCATIONAL LIMITED
LONDON

First published 1982.

Typeset by
and printed in Great Britain by
Billing & Son Ltd
London, Guildford & Worcester
for the publishers
Batsford Academic and Educational Ltd
an imprint of B T Batsford Ltd
4 Fitzhardinge Street
London W1H 0AH

British Library Cataloguing in Publication Data

Madge, Nicola
Ask the children: experiences of physical disability
in the school years.
1. Handicapped children—Education—Personal
narratives
I. Title   II. Fassam, Meg
371.9   LC3991

ISBN 0 7134 1896 6

ASK THE CHILDREN

Contents

Acknowledgements

This study was carried out within the scope of a broader project, concerned with services for disabled children and their families, funded by the Department of Health and Social Security and directed by Dr Chris Kiernan at the Thomas Coram Research Unit, University of London Institute of Education. We would like to express our gratitude to all concerned for this support, and to Andy Blanchard, who drew the pictures used in Chapter 8. In addition we wish to acknowledge many friends and colleagues for the helpful discussions we have had over the study period.
We would like to extend particular thanks to the children we talked to, who made data collection both fun and interesting, and to the schools and the Education Department involved for their encouragement and friendly cooperation.

1 Introduction

What does it *really* mean to be young and disabled? We decided to ask the children.

Surprisingly, this is an unusual approach. Most of what is written on childhood disability is based on the observations and points of view of professionals, practitioners and parents. Accounts from these perspectives are numerous and rich in detail. On the professional and administrative side, for instance, there are many detailed discussions of various aspects of disability. In particular, the Court Report (1976) has examined the role of health services for children, including those with disabilities, and the Warnock Report (1978) has looked into the school placement of children with special educational needs. At the practitioner level, there is increasing mention in periodicals, booklets and books of the problems and issues of disability as viewed by teachers, social work staff, medical workers and so on (Furneaux, 1973; Stevenson and Parsloe, 1978; McMichael, 1971). Finally, there are many excellent texts on the parental view of children's abilities, attitudes to school, friendship patterns, family relationships and so on (see, for example, Carnegie UK Trust, 1964; Anderson and Spain, 1977; Burton, 1975; Hewett, 1970).

Rarely, however, are children's views on these matters examined directly. Some researchers have drawn conclusions on children's reactions to disability, their preference for playmates with or without physical impairments, and the effects of contact on the attitudes and expectations of the able-bodied towards those with severe disabilities. But few of these studies have given children the opportunity to express their feelings in their own words. Instead subjects have been asked to select pictures of children they like best, to name their best friends or to rate the disabled, in general or in particular, on scales relating to need for attention, physical weakness, and so on. These kinds of question, which channel children's responses, are unlikely to produce quite the same views on disability as are enquiries which allow young people to express themselves in their own words.

Indeed when disabled adults speak for themselves, a wealth of individual and personal detail emerges. Most published material in which opinions and feelings are expressed by the disabled is contained in autobiographies (eg. Brown, 1954; Deacon, 1974) but there are also a number of collections of writings, on themes such as women and disability (Campling, 1981) or the elderly, including the elderly disabled (Blythe, 1979), which draw heavily on direct quotations. In some cases what people say depends on their ability to put their

5

thoughts into writing, but in other instances discussions are tape-recorded and written down later.

It is perhaps surprising that the points of view of disabled children and young people are so poorly documented. Richardson (1972) reports a conversation with three young adults (a student, a psychologist and a lawyer) and the mother of a 17 year-old girl with the same disability, although, as he himself points out (Richardson, 1976), findings from this type of enquiry can be non-representative as 'there may be a tendency to select unusually intelligent, sensitive informants who may recognize behaviour of which others may not be aware.' A discussion group for teenagers with asthma is described elsewhere (Tinkelman et al, 1976), but although there is mention of the recurrent themes in their conversations, such as anger and fear, no detailed comments from these young people are provided. In addition, adolescents with spina bifida have been asked about various aspects of their lives, including employment and personal relationships, in order to see how counselling services should be improved (Scott et al, 1975; Dorner, 1976). Again, however, the reports of these studies give little of the flavour of what the young people actually said.

Two anthologies of drawings, poetry and prose by disabled children (Exley, 1981; Royal National Orthopaedic Hospital School, 1981), both published during the International Year of Disabled People, perhaps come closest to allowing physically disabled children to speak for themselves. However neither collection aims to investigate topics in depth, and neither provides the views of able-bodied children for comparison. The value of these anthologies, nonetheless, is that they do indicate that children will happily convey their feelings—if asked.

The possibility of talking to children does not, of course, mean that what they say is necessarily completely accurate. Young people tend to be highly impressionable and they are not always fully reliable so far as chronology and detail of events are concerned. Nevertheless they are not usually reticent and seem to like talking about themselves and their experiences. On balance it seemed that conversations with children were a good idea, particularly as pupil comments would provide useful insights for professional workers coming into contact with the young disabled—such as teachers with little experience of disability who are participating in integration schemes, or social workers with perhaps only one or two children with physical impairments among their clients.

One of the first questions we asked the disabled children was how much they knew about their own physical condition, and whether they had discussed their disability with their families, teachers, doctors and others. We had little idea of what the pupils' answers would be as there is not much reference to this issue in the literature—not surprisingly, as the viewpoints of children are so frequently ignored in accounts of their circumstances.

There is, by contrast, quite a lot written about the problems facing disabled children. The motor and self-help restrictions imposed upon the physically impaired have in particular been stressed, and these evidently vary according to the nature and severity of a condition. Moreover many parents have emphasized how restrictions on mobility make going out with friends, trips and social activities especially difficult. All the same the significance of such limitations to a particular child cannot be fully assessed unless that child is asked.

Statements about the emotional consequences of disability have also frequently been made. Generally these have received considerable emphasis. Anderson and Spain (1977), for instance, point out how disabled children can receive differential treatment. It would seem that children with spina bifida are often treated as younger than they really are because of their problems of incontinence, mobility, intellect and growth.

Many writers have pointed to the stigma and discrimination that the disabled can face. As Hilbourne (1973) comments, 'A handicapped person is disadvantaged not solely because of his discrete disabilities but because he is socially judged to be a different quality of person by virtue of his deficiency.' Goffman (1963) has written extensively on stigma, and he maintains that unusual bodily features are taken to imply something about the moral status of a person. He describes how people with visible disabilities can be worse off than those with invisible impairments, and this has been confirmed by Goldberg (1974) who found that children with an invisible but serious handicap (congenital heart disease) were better adjusted socially than others with a visible but non-serious impairment (facial burns).

On the whole, however, there is more conjecture than knowledge about how the young disabled react emotionally to their disabilities, and about the worries they are likely to have.

The education of the young disabled raises important questions, and the advantages and disadvantages of special and integrated ordinary education have been hotly debated. Although *Statistics of Education* shows that around twenty three and a half thousand delicate and physically disabled pupils currently receive education in special schools in England and Wales, it has been demonstrated that many physically disabled children can successfully join their able-bodied peers, at least for some activities, in ordinary schools (Anderson, 1973; Cope and Anderson, 1977).

Support for integration of some physically disabled children within ordinary schools has most recently come from the Warnock Report (1978). Recommendations were consolidated in the Education Act 1981, which noted that a child of five years or over has a learning difficulty if he has a significantly greater difficulty in learning than the majority of children of his age, or if he has a disability which either prevents or hinders him from making use of educational facilities of a kind generally provided in schools, within the area of the local authority concerned, for children of his age. It was further specified that special educational provision should be made available for pupils with special educational needs stemming from a learning difficulty. Nevertheless it was also stated that it is the duty of a local education authority to secure that such a child is educated in an ordinary school if the parents are in agreement, and if such education is compatible with his receiving the special educational provision that he requires, with the provision of efficient education for the children with whom he will be educated, and with the efficient use of resources.

In general it seems, from the literature, that integration is feasible *provided* that pupils are within the normal range of intellectual ability and if they can cope emotionally with the rough and tumble of ordinary school. However feasibility does not mean inevitable success, and it appears that the level of facilities and resources present in ordinary schools will in large measure determine their ability to support disabled pupils (Holdsworth and Whitmore, 1974; Loring, 1975).

The present study provides an excellent opportunity to examine children's views on education of the disabled as we talked not only to disabled children in both special and ordinary education, but also to able-bodied children who had and had not experienced physical disability in their midst. In addition, and particularly fortunately, our comparisons of special and ordinary education could be enhanced by the comments of pupils who had personally attended both kinds of school.

Parents and teachers often suggest that disabled children have more difficulties than others in making and maintaining friendships. Anderson (1973), for instance, showed that primary age physically impaired children had fewer friends, and were rated as less popular, than the non-disabled, especially if their disabilities involved brain damage. Neurologically impaired children were also far less likely than all others to have their choice of 'best friend' reciprocated. We decided, in the present study, to pursue some of these questions from the point of view of the children. We wished to find out whether friendship patterns seemed to be affected by schooling and/or disability, and whether there were differences between the separate groups of pupils in the extent to which they were able to go out, and meet friends, after school. In addition we were interested to ask children about any unkind behaviour they had experienced. In Anderson's study of primary school children, teachers and parents were asked to report on children's experiences of teasing, and we sought to discover what children themselves thought.

Besides school and social life, we wanted to hear what children had to say about their families and homes. The best information on these questions at present comes from some of the studies of parents already referred to and is very much from the parental viewpoint. Family leisure appears from these accounts to be markedly restricted by the presence of a physically disabled child, and in general there seem to be few opportunities for such children to go out without their families.

Finally we wondered if pupils had any ideas about what the future might hold in store for them regarding jobs, somewhere to live, and spouses and children. Many parents of disabled children report considerable anxiety about what will happen when they become unable to support their children any longer. These events were many years off for many of the pupils we spoke to, but we did think it interesting at least to find out if they had yet thought realistically about the future.

Although our main interest throughout the study was in the attitudes and experiences of physically disabled children, we were for many reasons also interested to hear the views of non-disabled children. First, we could learn more about the normality or otherwise of the pupils with impairments if we compared them with their able-bodied contemporaries. Second, if there is to be integration at school and in the community, it is important to discover how knowledgeable children in general are about disability and what they feel about mixing with the disabled. And third, what did those in integrated education see as the main advantages and disadvantages of mixed schooling, and in what ways had they been affected by their contacts with the disabled?

Talking to able-bodied children can help to illuminate the development of attitudes towards disability. Some studies have shown how, from a young age, children are very similar in their feelings towards persons and figures with certain forms of impairment (Richardson et al, 1961; Siperstein and Gottlieb, 1977). although others indicate that prolonged contact under favourable conditions helps children to regard their disabled peers more realistically (Rapier et al, 1973; Richardson, 1971). We do not examine these issues in any systematic fashion, but we are able to provide some incidental evidence on them.

In order to provide some contextual background to the children's comments, we briefly interviewed several members of staff at the special and the comprehensive schools—and we also talked to the social worker attached to the special school. In addition, the class teachers at the special school filled in two brief questionnaires for each pupil to give some idea of the range of abilities and behaviour found in this particular school.

The conversations with the pupils, which were tape-recorded with the children's permission, formed the main part of our study. As another source of information, however, most subjects were shown a series of six pictures illustrating hypothetical situations involving both disabled and non-disabled children and asked a few set questions. These Picture Tests allowed us to enquire about children's attitudes to disability less directly, and in particular to discuss topics that might not have arisen in discussion of their personal experiences.

Before turning to the findings of our study, we would like to stress that what follows are the comments made by children at a single point of time. We have tried to reproduce faithfully the content and flavour of our conversations, but we recognize that children may have been selective in what they said just as we have inevitably chosen to include some, but omit other, quotations. Moreover although we used a standard schedule throughout, we added individual questions for pupils as and when they seemed appropriate. Tables of data are presented, where possible, to highlight any trends that might exist, but it must be stressed that as the numbers of subjects involved in comparisons are usually small, any conclusions drawn remain tentative.

Finally, it should be noted that the findings of this study are parts of a whole. For convenience the discussion has been broken down into sections focussing mainly, for example, on school or friends, but these divides are essentially artificial. Childhood, whether for the disabled or the able-bodied, is not so much a collection of isolated contexts and attitudes as an interlocking jigsaw of events, relationships and experiences. Let the children speak for themselves.

9

A note on terminology
There is much sensitivity and debate about the terms that should be used when referring to the physically disabled. Harris (1971) has outlined an essentially uncontested distinction between an *impairment* ('lacking part or all of a limb or having a defective limb or having a defective organ or mechanism of the body which stops or limits getting about, working or self-care'), a *disability* ('the loss or reduction of functional ability') and a *handicap* ('the disadvantage or restriction of activity caused by disability'). While we believe that it is more important to report on the world as it is than to argue over terminology, we have tended to adopt this approach throughout this book, and on the whole we have chosen to make greatest use of the terms 'disability' and 'disabled' when referring to children whose physical functions are restricted.

Nevertheless, in special education terms children are often still considered as physically handicapped (even though the Education Act 1981 recommends use of the general description of 'special educational needs') and many pupils themselves fairly consistently refer to 'handicap' and the 'handicapped.' We have accordingly reflected these patterns of usage in our conversations with the children and at certain points in the following pages.

2 The schools and the children

Our study of the meaning and experience of physical disability took place in a single London borough. At the time of the investigation there were one special school and two secondary level comprehensive schools offering places to pupils with appreciable physical handicaps, and we talked to children from all these schools. In addition, and to place our findings in perspective, we also interviewed non-disabled pupils both in the two comprehensives and in an ordinary junior school in the locality. In the rest of this chapter we provide some further preliminary information on these schools and pupils.

The schools
Special education for the physically disabled from a fairly wide catchment area was provided by the school included in our study. Pupils at this school ranged from nursery to school-leaving age and manifested a wide range of single and multiple physical impairments. The school had functioned as a special school for over fifty years and, although not purpose-built, it was very suitable for children with mobility problems. Most facilities and classrooms were located on the ground floor, and physiotherapy, medical and social work services— as well as a swimming pool—were available at the school.

In the six or so years preceding our study there had been opportunities for some of the older disabled pupils on the special school roll to attend nearby large ordinary comprehensive schools. We thought it instructive and interesting to ask teaching staff at the various schools for their opinions on, and experiences of, integrating physically disabled and able-bodied pupils, and the next sections of this chapter concentrate on their comments. In particular we describe attitudes expressed during discussions with the head of the special school, one head and two deputy head teachers from the comprehensive schools, and the teacher responsible for liaising between these schools.

The development of the integration scheme
The formal policy of transferring selected secondary level pupils from special to ordinary education had rather informal origins. Prior to the official scheme, cooperation between the heads of the special school and one of the comprehensives had allowed some disabled pupils to join their able-bodied peers fairly regularly for activities such as art and craft. Nevertheless the scale of this early initiative was limited,

and the staff at the schools became enthusiastic to operate a formal extensive scheme. An experiment in greater integration was therefore planned. The local authority became involved, due to the financial implications, and a person was appointed to oversee the venture. During the six months preceding September 1972—when eight severely disabled 14 year-old pupils were transferred from the special to the ordinary school on a full-time basis—intensive liaison was carried out between the host school, the children selected for integration, their parents, and the able-bodied pupils already at the secondary school. A maximum effort was put into ensuring that everyone concerned was as prepared as possible for the changes that were to occur.

The scheme at this stage was definitely an experiment, and it was made very clear from the outset that it would be discontinued after six months if it proved unsuccessful. However, as none of the major problems forecast materialized, the scheme continued. By 1976 the first comprehensive school had about 15 disabled pupils on its roll, spread across the full age range, and it was thought that the school could take no more. At this date the second local comprehensive school became involved in the scheme.

At present, and since our discussions with the children, opportunities for integration have been extended to primary level pupils. There are no immediate plans for further changes in policy although it has been mooted that a more even spread of pupils across schools could be achieved if all schools, and not just those that volunteered, became involved in the integration scheme. Nevertheless the resource implications of this practice, coupled with the prediction of fewer children suitable for ordinary education in the future, make it likely that integration will become less rather than more widespread.

Selecting pupils for integration

The teachers we asked were all clear that only certain pupils can be integrated successfully into large, and often boisterous, ordinary comprehensive schools, if the children are not to be placed in a difficult and conspicuous position and if an unreasonable amount is not to be demanded of staff. High academic ability is not necessary for success, although children of considerably below average ability are not suitable candidates for normal schools. Most important, it seems, is that the child is well-adjusted socially (or likely to become so), able to integrate, and can, on the whole, get around the school independently. Nevertheless, as one head put it, 'at the end of the day it's a real *gut* decision, whether the kid has got the inner strength to cope with all the pressures'.

The practical arrangements for selection usually follow a preliminary informal case conference early in the year at which children who might be suitable for integration are suggested. If there is general consensus on the point, a formal procedure is initiated and a medical doctor, an educational psychologist, parents and the children themselves become involved in the assessment process. Parents have the right of veto at this stage, but at the schools in question this had been exercised only once—in the case of a child with a fast deteriorating condition.

In most cases, selection and preparation of the children appeared appropriate and it seemed that in only three instances had a wrong decision to transfer a child to a comprehensive school been made. In the first case, a fairly mobile pupil had found great difficulty in coping emotionally in a normal classroom and had become aggressive: upon transfer back to the special school his behavioural problems ceased. The second 'failure' was also due to a pupil's inability to integrate with other children and his consequent unhappiness: he was transferred to a residential school. And thirdly, a very mildly disabled pupil developed a severe school phobia when placed in the comprehensive school which was cured only when he was transferred back to the special school. In all three cases emotional problems, rather than the physical disability as such, provided the reason for the change in schooling.

Links between special and ordinary schools

Disabled pupils receiving their education in the ordinary comprehensive schools remain on the roll of the special school. This policy was adopted to make sure that the disabled pupils receive the support they need in terms of special transport, medical examinations, physiotherapy and occupational therapy—all of which are much easier to arrange through the special school. In addition, pupils retain the services of a liaison teacher and welfare staff.

On the whole staff did not feel that retention of links with the special school was a disadvantage. In practical day-to-day terms, teachers thought that pupils identified with the school they attended. In any case, links were becoming less strong as the comprehensive schools gained better facilities, such as a swimming pool. At one of the secondary schools pupils were allowed to decide whether or not they wanted to return to the special school for games if they were unable to participate in activities offered at the ordinary school—and not one opted to go back to their old school.

Effects on the special school

Integration schemes can enhance the intellectual and social opportunities of some disabled pupils, but they do at the same time affect the environment, nature and role of the special schools. Inevitably the range of capabilities shown by pupils remaining at such schools is reduced. At the special school in question this, however, did not mean that a conscious external examination policy was discontinued or that pupils were no longer encouraged to enter for CSEs where possible—although it was becoming necessary to rewrite the school curricula to place the emphasis more firmly on education for living and to make sure that independence training and leisure-time activities assumed a greater prominence.

Integration also leads to a changing role for staff at special schools. Increasingly they have to become teachers of the multiply handicapped and forego the benefits of teaching bright children. In some cases it seemed that changes of this kind had taken their toll on job satisfaction.

On the other hand, however, an awareness of the positive aspects of integration may have led indirectly to some benefits for special school pupils. More opportunities had been provided for these children to interact socially with other children on a regular basis. And, just before we spoke to the head of the special school, a group of disabled and non-disabled pupils had spent a whole week together and held a conference. According to the head 'it was a smashing week. It was absolutely super.'

The lessons learned

In the opinion of the head of the special school, the biggest plus of the integration scheme is that if children are asked if they want to come back they invariably say 'no'. No major disasters had occurred since the experiment was first begun, and the teachers to whom we spoke indicated that the advantages of integrating suitable pupils far outweighed the disadvantages.

Staff were, moreover, keen to point to benefits gained by themselves and non-disabled children. One head stressed that comprehensive education should mean what it said and provide for all sections of the community. For his own part, he commented:

> It makes you ask yourself some questions. When I first came here and everyone said 'handicapped unit' and all the rest of it, you tended to say 'marvellous, wonderful' and without realizing you're doing it you bend over backwards for those kids. You *always* stand and open the door and let the child through. Not sometimes, but *always* you would notice the handicapped child and say good morning or good afternoon. You might pass 50 others by with a grunt or a glare or something, but a smile or so for that child. And then, you stop and say to yourself, 'Come on, Jones, what are you doing? This isn't integration at all.'

Able-bodied pupils, it seemed, had sometimes benefited very directly from the scheme. Several had become involved in designing aids for the disabled, and this project had provided them with a purpose for visiting the special school and talking to physiotherapists and occupational therapists. Teachers felt that integration had moreover provided a form of social training, as pupils began to appreciate the nature and consequences of physical disability for young people like themselves. One respondent thought that this was particularly true in making children aware of the possible outcomes of road traffic accidents. On the whole teachers did not think there was much teasing in their schools and thought there was a general acceptance of, and helpfulness towards, disabled pupils by staff and pupils alike.

Despite these positive aspects of integration, the teachers we spoke to did specify certain conditions which made the success of a scheme more likely. It was generally felt that integration was best at as young an age as possible, and that the proportion of disabled pupils in a school should closely resemble their proportion in the community. Such pupils should also be well distributed within any school, both to avoid their becoming too noticeable and to facilitate their integration. Indeed one respondent was quite concerned at the way integrated pupils often relied on adults for support of various kinds. If integration is to be meaningful, he thought, it must lead children to spend most of their time with other children.

Even if all these conditions are fulfilled, however, an integration

14

scheme cannot be viable if there are insufficient resources available. This point was most strongly emphasized by all the school staff we spoke to. Most important are adequate staffing levels, as teachers cannot be expected to spend more time with disabled than other pupils. In the words of one head:

> I will welcome the pupils and I will welcome the growth of integration, always provided that our needs in terms of staffing are recognized, and I think that's fair.

Teachers, moreover, required support themselves if they were to be responsible for disabled pupils. They could find it difficult knowing how to react to a handicapped child while at the same time trying to set an appropriate example to the able-bodied pupils. In some instances they needed to know what a specific condition involved and what should be done in certain circumstances: in one school a couple of incontinent children had presented staff with particular problems. Lastly they needed to be aware of when exceptions should and should not be made. Teachers tried not to react differently to disabled pupils—but they inevitably sometimes did.

Apart from resources in terms of staff, resources to ease the mobility of children around the school are also necessary. The layout of the building, ramps and lifts are all important in this context. Good efficient transport was also viewed as critical to the smooth running of an integration scheme. Furthermore, resources to be able to provide disabled school-leavers and their parents with realistic advice for the future were emphasized as important.

Finally, it was noted by school staff that often the greatest obstacles to successful integration stemmed from organizational factors. Apart from difficulties concerning insurance, getting funds when necessary and so on, it was the view of one head that the scheme would in some ways work better if all schools were required to participate. If this were the case it would not be necessary to rely on the goodwill of schools which in turn can adopt the attitude that they are 'doing a favour' by taking disabled pupils. The venture has worked well in the schools we investigated because of mutual trust and cooperation between the staff, but if there had been less common sympathy it might have failed within the first six months.

The pupils

The subjects for the study were drawn from four schools. From the special school we talked to 46 of the 58 disabled pupils of above infant age, and in 33 cases we were also able to assess attitudes towards disability less directly via the Picture Tests. The age of these subjects ranged between six and 15 years, and 24 were girls while 22 were boys.

Two groups of children were selected from the comprehensive schools. The first comprised 13 of the 16 disabled pupils on the roll of the special school—six at one of the comprehensives and seven at the other—and the second was an able-bodied comparison group matched for age, sex and school class. In all, 26 children were accordingly interviewed and tested in the comprehensive schools. In both the two sub-samples subjects ranged from 11 to 17 years, and in each case the average age was around 14 years. We spoke to eight girls and five boys from each of these two groups.

Finally, 16 pupils at an ordinary primary school were included in the study to serve as a younger non-disabled comparison group. Two girls and two boys were selected from each of the top four years for this purpose. Ages therefore ranged from eight to 11 years, with an average of just over nine years. All children were both interviewed and given the Picture Tests.

In most of the analyses that follow, data are combined for girls and boys, and age is usually represented as junior (primary level) or senior (secondary level). These divisions mean that five sub-groups are usually distinguished, and these are: able-bodied juniors, able-bodied seniors, disabled juniors in special education, disabled seniors in special education, and disabled seniors in integrated education.

Patterns of disability

One question of interest concerns the disabilities shown by the children in our study. In *The Health of the School Child* (1972) it was found that, overall in England and Wales, the largest groups of physically disabled children in special schools were, in order, those with cerebral palsy, spina bifida, heart diseases and muscular dystrophy. By comparison the physically disabled in ordinary schools most commonly suffered from, again in order, congenital abnormalities, heart diseases, cerebral palsy and spina bifida.

A rather different picture was found for the children in our study. As Table 1 shows, not too dissimilar patterns of disability existed within the three groups comprising junior pupils in special education, senior pupils in special education and senior pupils in ordinary education. Cerebral palsy and spina bifida were most common in all groups, and muscular dystrophy occurred twice in both the senior special and the senior ordinary education sub-samples. Road traffic accident victims seemed to be concentrated within special education, but, for the variety of other handicaps present within the sample, numbers were too small to discern any significant patterns. In general then, although bearing in mind that the numbers of children involved were small, there is no evidence that, within our sample, type of impairment influenced schooling for the physically disabled.

We also examined the numbers of disabled boys and girls in the different types of schools, and a number of interesting findings are shown in Table 2. First, it is noted that there was, overall, a slight preponderance of girls over boys: this is a common finding among populations of the disabled. Second, there was some indication that among senior pupils it was girls who were more likely than boys to be found in integrated schools. Although this difference did not reach statistical significance, it did at least suggest that girls were more often able than boys to cope with normal education. Quite why this was so, however, remains an open question.

The schools and the children

Disability	Junior pupils	Senior pupils	
	Special education	Special education	Ordinary education
Cerebral palsy	11	7*	3**
Spina bifida	9	4	4
Muscular dystrophy	—	2	2
Road traffic accidents	2	2	—
Arthrogryphosis	2	—	1
Congenital heart	1	1	—
Amputation	1	—	—
Congenital malformation	1	—	—
Brittle bones	—	—	1
Epilepsy	—	1	—
Hydrocephalus	1	—	—
Polio	—	—	1
Sickle cell anaemia	—	—	1
Ureterostomy	1	—	—

*One pupil additionally suffered from sickle cell anaemia

**One pupil additionally suffered from epilepsy

Table 1: Category of disability by school placement and age

Sex	Junior pupils	Senior pupils		Total
	Special education	Special education	Ordinary education	
Male	12	10	5	27
Female	17	7	8	32
Total	29	17	13	59

Table 2: Physically disabled children by school placement and age

Aids and appliances

Impaired mobility affected a number of physically disabled pupils, and the children who used various aids and appliances are indicated in Table 3.

Nearly half the disabled juniors in special education did not use any form of aid to mobility. Three of the remainder were in wheelchairs and the rest used walking aids such as calipers, crutches or a rollator.

There were some contrasts in the use of aids between disabled seniors in special education and those integrated into comprehensive schools. In particular it is interesting to note that just over a third of the first, but almost two-thirds of the second group, used aids, and that a slightly larger proportion of the pupils in ordinary education used wheelchairs. In other words, it is evident that considerably restricted mobility, or the use of a wheelchair, did not prevent placement in ordinary education.

Characteristics of group	Wheelchairs		Other walking aids		Other		None		Total
	No.	% of group	No.	% of group	No.	% of group	No.	% of group	No.
Juniors in special education	3	10.3	11	37.9	1	3.4	14	48.3	29
Seniors in special education	4	23.5	3	17.6	0	—	10	58.8	17
Seniors in integrated education	4	30.8	4	30.8	0	—	5	38.5	13
Total	11	18.6	18	30.5	1	1.7	29	49.2	59

Table 3: Use of aids and appliances

Neurological impairment

The head teacher at the special school was asked to indicate whether pupils in our sample were definitely, possibly, or definitely not neurologically impaired, and the findings are shown in Table 4. As can be seen, it is only among the seniors in integrated education that the majority of children definitely had no neurological impairment.

Earlier experiences of ordinary education

It should also be pointed out that not all pupils classified as physically disabled had spent all their school days in either special or integrated provision. It transpired that 12 of the 46 children currently attending the special school had at some stage been pupils at ordinary schools, and that for four of the 13 older children integrated at local comprehensive schools, their current school was not their first experience of ordinary education.

Characteristics of group	Definitely neurologically impaired		Possibly neurologically impaired		Not neurologically impaired		Total
	No.	% of group	No.	% of group	No.	% of group	No.
Juniors in special education	14	48.3	11	37.9	4	13.8	29
Seniors in special education	11	64.7	4	23.5	2	11.8	17
Seniors in integrated education	2	15.4	3	23.1	8	61.5	13
Total	27	45.8	18	30.5	14	23.7	59

Table 4: Neurological impairment

It is of interest to look in whatever detail possible at the circumstances of these 16 children on whose behalf a decision had at some time been taken to transfer them from an ordinary to a special school (although in the case of the four comprehensive school pupils, transfer back had since occurred). A first consideration is their primary disabilities and these are shown in Table 5.

Disability	No. of pupils
Cerebral palsy	6
Muscular dystrophy	4
Road traffic accident	3
Spina bifida	2
Epilepsy	1
Total	16

Table 5: Primary disabilities of pupils initially in ordinary education

It emerged that there were two main reasons why children were transferred from ordinary to special schools. The first, as might be expected, is that a proportion of the severely disabled became physically impaired during early childhood. Of the 16 children under consideration, this was so for the four muscular dystrophy cases, the three victims of road traffic accidents, the child with epilepsy and at least one of the pupils with cerebral palsy. In other words, over half these children were not born disabled. And the second was that some children found it difficult to cope amongst non-disabled pupils. In the words of one girl who had recently joined the special school,

I didn't feel like going to that school (i.e. an ordinary school) because they usually pick on you, and so I felt like coming to this school.

Abilities and behaviour in the special school

The pupils at the special school are a group for whom opportunities for integration are not available or for whom, among the older pupils, transfer to an ordinary school has not been recommended. General information on these children was provided by their class teachers and this can be used to gain a clearer picture of their characteristics and, in particular, to see the degree to which pupils tend to resemble one another. Unfortunately this information is available only for pupils attending the special school—so the different sub-groups of children in the study cannot be contrasted—but for these subjects it is fairly comprehensive and covers both abilities and behaviour at school.

The data are based on ratings made by class teachers on the Questionnaire for Teachers of Special Children* which generated information on subjects' abilities in five main areas relevant to the school situation: self-help, communication, ability to occupy self, physical skills and educational attainments. Full and partial SCOPE scores (each letter in SCOPE referring to one of the areas of ability listed above) were derived from assessments on 15 items, which were comprised of three questions on each of the five areas, as below:

S (self-help)
—Does (the pupil) feed self?
—Does (the pupil) dress self?
—Does (the pupil) wet self during day?
C (communication)
—Can (the pupil) use language normally?
—Is it easy to understand what (the pupil) says?
—Does (the pupil) understand if asked or told to do something?
O (ability to occupy self)
—How much of the time does (the pupil) need to be watched to make sure he/she doesn't get into danger or create a disturbance?
—Does (the pupil) demand much attention in the school situation?
—How good is (the pupil) at concentrating on a particular task?
P (physical ability)
—Does (the pupil) have any difficulty walking (with calipers or other aid if used)?
—Can (the pupil) go up and down stairs?
—Can (the pupil) do fiddly things with his/her hands such as using scissors or holding a pencil properly?
E (educational skills)
—How much can (the pupil) read and understand?
—Can (the pupil) count and use numbers appropriately?
—Can (the pupil) express him/herself in writing?

*devised by one of the authors for use with a wide group of children in special education

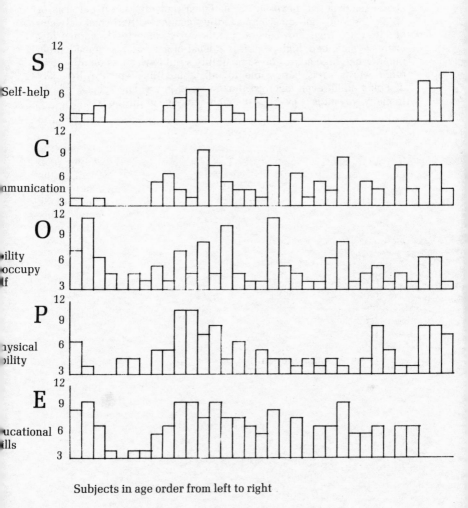

Subjects in age order from left to right

Figure 1: SCOPE scores of special school pupils

Four alternative responses could be selected for each question and these were associated with scores of (1) (no disability) to (4) (severe disability).

Figure 1 presents, graphically, the scores of individual children—arranged in age order from left to right—on the SCOPE scale. Two main observations can be made on the ratings. First it can be seen that age seemed not to have strong or consistent effects on patterns of ability. Second, and most importantly, immense differences between children are revealed: several pupils fairly consistently gained low scores, some had high scores on most items, and a considerable number had high scores on some abilities but low scores on others. In other words, it is impossible to talk about the 'typical' physically disabled child, even amongst those placed in a single special school. In many ways this is perhaps the main message of this book.

3   Disability and its meaning

Disability has many meanings and in this chapter we look at these for both able-bodied and disabled pupils. In the case of the non-disabled we enquire about knowledge of people with physical impairments and handicaps, and in the case of the disabled we examine understanding and discussion of personal disability, experiences of hospital, and the effects of disability upon physical skills, social activities and relationships, and worries.

Knowledge of other people's disability
Just over half of the junior pupils in the ordinary primary school reported some degree of contact with one or more disabled people. This proportion is, not surprisingly, less than that found for the able-bodied seniors, all of whom were in daily contact with the physically disabled pupils integrated in their classes. Table 6 presents these findings.

Characteristics of group	Disabled person(s) known		Disabled person(s) not known		Total
	No.	% of group	No.	% of group	No.
Able-bodied juniors	9	56.3	7	43.8	16
Able-bodied seniors	13	100.0	0	0	13
Total	22	75.9	7	24.1	29

Table 6: Able-bodied pupils' knowledge of disabled person(s)

How well disabled people were known, nonetheless, varied between the children and we were interested, especially in relation to younger pupils in normal education, to learn more about acquaintances. As Table 7 shows, most people who claimed to know someone with a physical impairment could give a reasonable description of symptoms, although considerably fewer were aware of clinical diagnosis. It was, as would be expected, the senior pupils who were most knowledgeable about medical labels.

From the children's descriptions, it emerged that six of the primary school pupils had come across disability through contact with the disabled children of friends, relatives or neighbours. In some of these cases rather clear descriptions of the disabilities involved were given.

23

An eight year-old girl, for example, told us

> This girl, my auntie, she's got a daughter, and her daughter's handicapped and she's fifteen. And she's small, she's ill ... She can't walk and she has to stay in bed all day. She can't half sit down.

while a nine year-old boy said

> My mate's mum, right. She's got a child and he's handicapped. He can't speak properly. I don't think he can write.

Occasionally it seemed that the children's accounts were reliant more on what they had been told than what they had witnessed for themselves, and in this way the power of a 'handicap' label was evident. Two children in particular seemed to think that they knew someone who was disabled, although they were less than clear as to what this meant. In one of these instances a child explained

> My friend's sister—she lives next door to me. Her brother told me that she's handicapped. I don't know what's wrong with her.

whereas in the other the pupil commented that

> My mum's friend's daughter: she can walk but she's handicapped.

Some children, by contrast, gave rather good interpretations of disability, and we were especially impressed by the comments of a ten year-old boy who said of his cousin

> She's mongol, so she's about two months behind her actual age—she's five.

Despite a slight misunderstanding of developmental norms, he clearly had quite a sophisticated idea of disability. Indeed this description of his cousin served to put his earlier definition of handicap into perspective:

> Handicap—there's two ways I know it. Some people can't do special things and some people—I believe we have 21 or 41 something, but some handicapped people have another one more than us in our features.*

Of the remaining three primary school pupils who claimed to have some direct experience of disability, one mentioned his acquaintance with a boy he sometimes met on the coach or at a local playscheme, another described two children—one who went to his brother's school and had been pointed out by him, and the other whom he met at a playscheme—and the third told us about a friend she played with in her local park. In all these instances the respondents could describe the physical characteristics of the disabled children they told us about, although this was usually the extent of their knowledge.

Indeed it has already been pointed out how rarely the primary school children made any comments about causality, or clinical diagnoses, of disability. Some children had words like 'spastic' at the forefront of their vocabularies, but during our discussions only two apparently used disability labels at all correctly: one of these was the boy who reported his cousin's mongolism, and the other was a girl who cited the much more easily-comprehended condition of deafness.

*He was evidently referring to the chromosomal abnormality characterizing Down's Syndrome (mongolism).

| Characteristics of group | Description of symptoms | | Clinical diagnosis | | Total |
| | Given for disabled person(s) known* | | | | |
	No.	% of group	No.	% of group	No.
Able-bodied juniors	7	43.8	2	12.5	16
Able-bodied seniors	11	84.6	6	46.2	13
Total	18	62.1	8	27.6	29

*Subjects are included if they can cite symptoms/diagnosis of at least one disabled person.

Table 7: Knowledge of symptoms and clinical diagnosis of disabled person(s)

Apart from knowing particular disabled people, some of the junior school respondents clearly had a more general awareness of disability and its meaning. Sometimes children mentioned relevant television programmes they had seen—viewed either at home or school—and one boy said that he had come across disabled children as his mother helped out on a special school bus. Nevertheless, children's comments need to be interpreted cautiously: one pupil who had seemed particularly alerted to issues of handicap during the interview finally admitted that he had received prior warning about what we were going to talk about:

> So when Sheila was coming down the stairs she told me. She said it was something about handicaps and other people that mix up schools ... in a mixed-up school.(!)

In contrast to the junior school children, all the non-disabled seniors in our study had at least passing acquaintance with physically disabled people, even if only with the pupils integrated into their comprehensive schools. As the able-bodied and disabled pupils at these schools were drawn from the same classes, the non-disabled subjects encountered physical disability daily at school, a fact which they all pointed out.

All the same this did not mean that these seniors had full knowledge of the symptoms and diagnoses of their peers, as Table 7 shows. Most could describe well the physical limitations of their fellow pupils, but only about half could specify the physical condition from which any of the disabled pupils in the school suffered. Those who did name specific diagnoses mentioned polio, brittle bones, thalidomide, heart trouble and spina bifida. Amongst those who did not know about medical conditions, however, were some children who were not interested in knowing, or who did not feel it was any of their business. This last sentiment was expressed by two girls, of 14 and 17 years, whose comments in relation to clinical diagnosis of their friends were

I don't really ask, because I don't really think it's good enough to ask people 'why?' and 'what?'

and

'I don't know because I haven't asked her'.

This, however, was not a universal attitude and some pupils were very much aware not only of diagnosis but also of causality. Half of subjects interviewed introduced notions of cause into their descriptions of disabled peers and acquaintances, and the effects of illness and disease, birth hazards, accidents and congenital malformations were all mentioned. An illustration of a knowledgeable and sophisticated approach to disability is provided by a 14 year-old girl's clinical description of her friends at school in which she stated

I don't know the name of anything, but G ..., she hasn't got any kneecaps, and S ..., she was born like that from birth and she's got operations on her feet, and she told me she was born with her back open, so she had to have it stitched up but then it was open and so they had to stitch it up again. A girl called L ..., she sort of limps, and she has to use crutches. And there is this boy, A ..., and he has to use crutches probably all the time I think. And I think he's lost the use of his legs, sort of a little bit.

Evidently knowledge and understanding of disability differs between children, and it would seem to be affected by a number of factors. Contact with disabled people, first of all, is important as evidenced by the contrasting experiences of most juniors in normal education and the seniors at comprehensive schools involved in the integration scheme. Secondly, age is undoubtedly influential too, as witnessed by the differences in the general sophistication of accounts typically offered by these two groups of pupils. Thirdly, degree of acquaintance or friendship is also contributory and may be critical—certainly some of the junior pupils were considerably influenced by their knowledge of disabled people outside the context of school. And of fourth significance, although easier to speculate about than to quantify, are the personal interests and attitudes of children: the differences between some of the senior pupils in their willingness to label and discuss the problems of their disabled peers

Characteristics of group	Personal diagnosis known		Some idea of cause of personal disability		Total
	No.	% of group	No.	% of group	No.
Juniors in special education	7	24.1	7	24.1	29
Seniors in special education	8	47.1	5	29.4	17
Seniors in integrated education	11	84.6	8	61.5	13
Total	26	44.1	20	33.9	59

Table 8: Physically disabled pupils' knowledge of personal diagnosis and cause of disability

pay at least partial testimony to this claim.

Knowledge of personal disability

To find out how much the physically disabled pupils in our sample knew about their own clinical condition, its cause and prognosis, we asked them if they could name and describe their impairment. As can be seen from Table 8, most seniors in integrated education, half the seniors in special education, and only a quarter of the junior special pupils, knew the medical label commonly given to their condition. The disabled seniors in ordinary education were the most able to offer some indication of the causes of their disability.

Not only did subjects differ in their ability to name their own physical condition, but they also showed marked contrasts in the amount of detail they could provide and in their apparent concern for such knowledge. Among those who did not seem very bothered about the technicalities of their diagnosis was, for instance, a 15 year-old boy with spina bifida who said his disability was

> Just physical handicap. Just say I was born like that and that's as far as I take it.

Indeed a few children, especially those at the special school, seemed quite surprised at being asked if their disability had a name, one replying 'No. Why?' and another stating emphatically 'Oh no, not yet'.

Nevertheless, as already indicated, there were many children who seemed very knowledgeable about their condition. One 14 year-old commented:

> I think it's called spinal muscular atrophy. I think, I'm not sure though. I think that's the name.

and added that it meant

> Weakness of muscles in my back. My back's bending, it's crooked because the muscles in my back aren't strong enough to keep me straight.

Likewise another boy of about the same age, whilst claiming that his diagnosis was unimportant to him, could all the same give a good account. Having told us that his condition was called spina bifida, he went on to say

> I don't know (how it happened), I'm not sure. People keep telling me but I'm not very interested, I don't care really ... Something about my back, not a hole in my back, but a nerve came out of my back or something and they had to take it down and stitch it up and things like that. Something about my back — and then I've got a valve in my head. That's all they've explained.

Needless to say not all children were as articulate about their disability, although many did have at least some idea of its nature. A 13 year-old girl did not specifically say that she had brittle bones although she reported that

> I was born weak and I fell down the stairs and I broke my leg and after that I kept breaking it.

which, after all, is probably an accurate description of her physical condition. Somewhat by contrast, another female pupil of the same age could give herself a clinical label — although it clearly meant little

27

to her. When asked what her disability was called she retorted

> Spasticity. But I don't like that. My mum don't. She had to go down the hospital once and a doctor said 'her legs have got spasticity' and my mum goes 'I don't like that. Why don't you say handicapped?'. And he said 'that's the proper name for it'.

More practically, however, she described her symptoms as including

> Pains in my joints—side, top of my legs. Sometimes, say when I'm walking, I might collapse...

Quite a number of children did not think of their difficulties as neatly fitting a label. A 13 year-old cerebral palsied boy asked about his diagnosis remarked

> How do you mean? I don't quite understand, you see. Nobody has explained to me, no. I don't know about that.

although he was well able to give an account of his physical shortcomings:

> I seem to lose my strength. When I pick up a chair to put round the table I seem to ... it sort of hurts. When I go up the stairs I go up so slow dragging my feet. It hurts my back when I bend. When I jump, well I can't jump very high. (When I'm out for a walk) I sort of start to drag my feet along the floor, I have to have a rest. I keep thinking I haven't got a proper heart. That's what I keep thinking—the way I keep losing my breath and stuff.

All in all children showed enormous variability in the information they could provide on their physical conditions, although the vast majority were willing to provide as good a description as they could. Much the same kind of conclusion can be drawn regarding the reasons respondents gave for their disabilities: whereas some children were very straightforward and matter-of-fact in their descriptions of how they had become disabled, others seemed to have a rather confused and probably invalid idea, while others still had no insights or thoughts about the matter.

Of course it is very often difficult, if not impossible, to establish the cause of disability and children were not expected to give highly technical and detailed accounts. The descriptions of spinal muscular atrophy and spina bifida already described were, for instance, regarded as providing some indication of cause although the commonly-heard claim 'I was just born like it' was not.

Some children's limited idea about the cause of their disability reflected a real lack of knowledge, even on the part of doctors. For some subjects, such as a 15 year-old girl with spina bifida and hydrocephalus at one of the comprehensive schools, this seemed a matter of considerable concern. She commented many times that she wished she knew more about why she had spina bifida, and said on one occasion

> I'd like to know what caused it. My mum had four healthy children before and then she had me and then she had a little boy who died. All the years I've been thinking he was handicapped but he wasn't—he collapsed—his heart—and they got to the theatre too late. I want to know why she had four normal, one handicapped and one normal again. I thought that if she had any after me they'd be handicapped as well, but they weren't. I know we can't all be normal, but I'd like to know what causes it.

Certain possible causes had been through her mind, but on the whole these had been rejected:

> My sister knows this guy and he says that in Ireland, many years ago, it's because they eat potatoes* So I told my mum and she says its a load of rubbish... You know you take tablets for your head and stuff, and people smoke. My mum, she smokes once in a while, but I realize it's got nothing to do with that. My mum used to smoke, but when she had me and my other sisters and brothers she stopped smoking because the doctor told her to... Then one day she had me — an ugly looking thing, so I was told, with a hole in my back and everything. And as I grew up I kept asking what was wrong with me.

Nevertheless it seemed, in this girl's case, that she suspected that the severity of her disability might have been avoided.

> I would have been alright if it wasn't for the doctor. I blame him for what happened to me. When I was born I had a hole in my back, quite a big one. They shut that and then something else went wrong and they didn't fix it right away, so from that one thing led to another. That's why I'm like this. Otherwise I'd have been alright, so I'm told.

Despite not necessarily being able to give lucid accounts, some subjects did give what appeared to be plausible explanations of their personal disability. This applied to an integrated pupil who had suffered from polio and told us:

> I've got no idea (why I contracted polio) — and there's different stories what I hear. That I went to one country and I forgot to take the injection and I just caught it like that.

and to the 11 year-old cerebral palsied special school pupil who maintained:

> Well I'm premature, right, and the doctors gave me too much oxygen and it made me handicapped.

Although many children volunteered reasons for their disability, it was not always clear how accurate these were. A 14 year-old epileptic girl told how

> I was slightly disabled from when I was born. I had difficulty in breathing — I'm a twin, and my brother's bottom was in my face, so I couldn't breathe properly so there was some damage in my brain.

Whether or not her account was correct she, like many other pupils, had her own idea of why she thought she was disabled.

As might be expected, the most comprehensive understanding of the causes of disability was shown by the oldest and most mature of the integrated pupils — although it is of interest to note how, even in these cases, information had not always been easy to come by. A pupil with cerebral palsy, and falling within this category, explained

> Well, up to a couple of years ago I didn't know exactly what it was. But then I found out. It's like a blockage in part of my brain which controls my muscles in my legs, and since my brain couldn't operate my muscles properly and get them to move as it wanted them to, they just grew weaker

*A second child, also suffering from spina bifida, told us 'My mum says it happened because of too many potatoes or something. Potatoes weren't washed too good'.

and weaker and they don't know how to work. They'll never be able to do it to a 100 per cent degree, but hopefully they'll be able to do it to a high degree.

Another girl, too, commented on how she had only recently discovered the origins of one of her two disabilities.

> I've only known recently...that sickle cell anaemia is hereditary, that both my family in fact made me worse. And they are both carriers of sickle cell anaemia and now I've got a bigger dose. And I only found that out recently...It's only recently they've started to help me with my blood. I mean why couldn't they have done that in the third year when it could have helped me most? Maybe I'd have had some 'O' levels by now.

It is difficult to generalize about the findings presented in this section other than to remark that the integrated older pupils were more knowledgeable than the others about their personal disabilities. Among the special school pupils only about half the seniors, and far fewer juniors, could name their clinical condition and only one in three of the seniors had any idea concerning its cause.

Talking about disability

During the course of conversation we asked pupils about opportunities they had for talking about their disability, and about what was said on such occasions. The overwhelming impression given by the children was that not much discussion of disability took place.

Only 15 out of 58 children with physical disabilities claimed that they ever spoke to their parents about their disabilities and within this small group there were still considerable differences in both the nature and extent of any such discussions that did occur. For some of these children it appeared that the main focus of conversation was on parents telling their children more about their condition, and why it had apparently happened. One boy said that his father told him, when he was about two years old, that he had got spina bifida, and that he had later explained in more detail what had occurred.

Other subjects, too, were appreciative of their parents. One boy with muscular dystrophy said his father was very honest with him, and a special school pupil told how her parents

> ...talk to me about anything really. Anything that I ask they tell me. So really I know about me and about other people and, well, about what I ought to know really.

Quite what was discussed by a ten year-old spina bifida boy and his parents was, however, never made explicit. Although he indicated that disability as a topic did occasionally pop up, sometimes initiated by him and sometimes by his parents, he would comment only 'official secret' when asked what kind of things were talked about.

Some pupils who did not indicate that they ever spoke to their parents about their disability nonetheless almost certainly had good communicative relationships. Sometimes it seemed that the topic never really came up in a strict sense. One girl remarked that 'in my family they don't count me handicapped', and a boy with muscular dystrophy commented

> I don't think that we talk about it. It's not that it's nothing bad or anything. It's just that it never crops up.

adding, when asked if he would tell his parents if anyone was particularly unpleasant to him,

> No, I wouldn't do that. I suppose if I do I think of myself as a bit of a coward. I try and get over it myself. I try and do it myself. That's the main reason.

On other occasions however, interpersonal difficulties were apparent, and one integrated pupil at a comprehensive school said of her mother

> She's like them here, she don't care. I say she don't care, I don't think she does. If I talk to her she just don't bother listening. I tell her people tease me at school, but she says it's good for me... You just get the feeling she don't care. So every time there's a meeting at school I just forget about it 'cos I know she ain't going to come.

Much the same kind of frustration seemed to be experienced by a male pupil at the special school who rarely spoke to his parents when he was worried because 'they're too busy and they say "what are you on about?".'

Another reason for lack of family discussion of disability seemed to result from a reluctance, however derived, on the part of the subject to bring certain matters into the open. One pupil specifically mentioned that she did not talk to her mother for fear of upsetting her, and another claimed that he did not tell his parents what was worrying him but just kept things to himself.

Even fewer children claimed to discuss their disability with brothers and sisters than said they talked with parents. In some cases, however, a sibling did seem to provide some substitute for a non-communicative mother or father, and both the two pupils last referred to said that they occasionally talked to their sister and brother respectively. Nevertheless in the former case it did not seem that the sister was a totally satisfactory outlet, as our subject commented that

> Sometimes I just feel like saying everything, you know, how I feel, but I just don't say it.

Unsurprisingly brothers and sisters sometimes proved to be particularly annoying, and in these instances there was little chance of sympathetic communication. A 15 year-old special school pupil with spina bifida provided such an illustration when talking about his ten year-old brother:

> I'm always getting cross with him because he doesn't do as I say. I mean he's got to help me in some ways...Mum says it's because he doesn't understand, but I mean he should understand by that age, shouldn't he? I mean I understanded everything when I was about his age — everything my Mum told me I understood. I think he understands that I did...But just because I'm like this I think he has to help me a little bit more. If I can't lift something, if I can't do something, he's got to help me more you know. But he doesn't. Every time I ask him he just says 'no' and it ends up being a fight.

There was apparently also little understanding at home for another special school pupil. Besides, in his view, having uninterested parents, he claimed that he came in for considerable teasing about his various disabilities from his brothers who called him 'handy' (short, apparently, for handicapped).

Not all pupils, however, wished or needed to discuss their disability with brothers or sisters—or indeed counted normal conversation about everyday issues, which might have been about practical problems, as 'talking about disability'. This is illustrated by one girl who, when asked whether she talked about such matters with her brothers and sisters, said:

> Funnily enough, no, I don't know why, but we don't. When I'm round with them I forget I'm handicapped—I think I'm me. It's the way I've been brought up really.

We also asked children if they had discussed their disabilities to any extent with doctors. The answers we gained suggested that it was only with the older and more sophisticated pupils (mostly those in the integration scheme) that conversations of this kind had taken place. Often it seemed that where discussions with doctors had occurred, these had been largely at the instigation of the respondent. A female pupil with cerebral palsy, who had only recently discovered the cause of her disability, said that her policy was

> Just ask, you know. I just ask away and see whether I get the answer.

Another pupil, who had also found out about her condition only recently, had become intent on getting more and more information from her doctor. On the whole she found medical staff helpful, although she admitted that she did not always understand what they said. Nevertheless having discovered quite a lot about her sickle cell anaemia, she now planned to learn about other aspects of her disability:

> I'm trying to find out what they can do about my limp and what they can do about fitting me with a new joint because at the moment I can't bend my leg because the joints in that leg are stiff...Then they explained to me that if they give me an artificial joint and it got infected...then they would have to take it out and then they'll have to fuse both bones together because they can't put the bone they took out back, so my leg would be even shorter. I've only found that out recently. They don't approach you, you have to ask them. You have to go on asking.

In relation to the blood transfusions she had only just begun to have, she claimed

> It's only because I've talked about it a great deal recently and told them 'Look, I have a lot of pain, what's going to happen to me when I start working?' that they decided to start some treatment.

From the limited evidence available it did seem that, in the experience of the children in this study, professional discussion of disability was restricted to the most articulate pupils. However this does not mean that the more shy children did not notice this lack of consultation. Indeed its absence was specifically pointed out by a 14 year-old with arthrogryphosis who explained that

> The doctors told my brother-in-law what happened and my brother-in-law told me, you know, what's wrong with me. But the doctors never told me. Like if I go there's a lot of doctors there. They look at me, they talk among themselves, they never talk to me.

All the same, it is no doubt true that many children were satisfied with their contacts with members of the medical profession. Several mentioned, in passing, comments made by doctors about their progress and prognosis. In the words of a boy with muscular dystrophy

> Oh yeah, they've answered me straight. Because I'd rather know. Like they say this disease could last you 16 years or it could last you 30, they reckon. I don't take any notice of that. I mean it's only an estimation. I mean I could die tomorrow—you know, crossing the road. If a bus hits me I'm dead anyway. So you just take it like that. So just make the most of the life you've got.

Very occasionally pupils mentioned discussions of disability with professionals other than doctors such as teachers, physiotherapists or the social worker. However, it did seem that many children in the sample had very few outlets for talking about aspects of disability that worried them, or for asking questions to which they would have liked answers. Parents and siblings were able to fulfil this role for some pupils, but for others it did not seem that the gap was adequately filled in any way.

Hospitalization

The comments made by children that have already been quoted in this chapter go some way towards illustrating the very direct physical consequences of disability. In this section we present a selection of descriptions given by subjects of their stays in hospital. In all cases comments arose spontaneously during conversations, and as such the experiences referred to may or may not be respresentative of those of the sample as a whole.

Thirteen of the children volunteered during interview that they had had operations of some kind or another, and several more reported stays in hospital for other reasons. Sometimes these experiences had come to be fairly routine, as in the case of an eight year-old boy suffering from ureterostomy who provided a detailed chronology of his operations:

> I had one when I was born, I had one when I was two months old, had one when I was nine months old, had one when I was one, had one when I was two, had one when I was three, had one when I was four...No, I had four, I mean I had five, then I had one when I was seven and when I was eight. I've got to have two more, maybe in April. They said it was going to be in March—I haven't heard yet.

He continued

> They say the operation is for to make it better and so that you can go to an ordinary school. I said I don't want an operation and I don't want to go to ordinary school. They said you must have one. I said alright. On Monday morning I went in the theatre, one minute ago she put an injection in me, one second ago I was flashed, asleep.

Some children clearly had rather mixed feelings about being in hospital. One of the pupils in the sample was a ten year-old boy who had only very recently been involved in a road traffic accident. Despite his trauma, which he described in fairly graphic detail, a big grin came over his face when asked what it had been like in hospital and he replied, simply, 'Fun'. An eight year-old girl with cerebral palsy was also evidently more impressed with the incidentals of hospital life—although at the same time she seemed to have a reasonable idea of the point of her operation. She related how

> When I couldn't walk I was in hospital, and I went in that room [she earlier said that she had had her operation in a big green room] to have the plaster on my leg, and the stick between it, and the nurse was very kind. She gave me a boiled egg, and a tea, and a toast. She took the stick off and the plaster off and she...put a drill. And I sat up, I didn't see nothing done through my leg. She just got the plaster off my leg, and broke the stick. It's a bit of wood.

Also suffering from cerebral palsy, a slightly older girl similarly gave a light-hearted description of the time surrounding her operation:

> And I was in hospital when I was eight in 1975...On my birthday I came out. I was with my mother then. She came and visited me and I was in my bed. Then when I was getting up out of bed, the porridge went right over me. And my brother-in-law and sister-in-law, they came up and visited me, and my sister-in-law came up and gave me a kiss.

Unfortunately, however, some respondents did not regard their hospitalizations with such equanimity. The girl quoted earlier who blamed the doctors for the severity of her spina bifida is a good example. Whether or not her claims were warranted, she needed recurrent spells in hospital, sometimes as a matter of life and death. She told us

> I go in about every two years when it (my valve) affects me and they change it. When I start to be sick and it starts hurting me, that's when I know it needs changing. Two years ago they said to my mum and my dad that if they'd left me a week later I'd have been dead—I was practically on the verge of it.

A second pupil with spina bifida also thought that an operation that failed to work contributed to her present physical state, although her understanding of the situation was much more accepting. Indeed her emotional attitude was markedly different from the feelings of a boy who laid the blame for his spasticity entirely at the door of medical services he had received. He was quite convinced that a visit to the dentist at age eight to have six teeth removed caused a stroke which in turn led to his collapse, his temporary inability to walk and his more long-term difficulties in fine motor control.

Most of the rest of the pupils who mentioned operations, and being in hospital, did so very straightforwardly, typically explaining that they had had a leg straightened, a hip 'done', or a valve or urinary diverson fitted. Respondents nonetheless differed in the degree of explanation offered, and some of the older pupils gave immensely technical accounts. Certainly the details related by a 15 year-old about an operation eight months previously fall into this category:

> I think it's bilateral triplearthedesis. They had to take some bones out of my feet and build up an arch to try to help my balance, and hopefully it will work. And they had to do another ETA, you know elongate the tendon...because I'd had it done quite a few years ago and they thought it was time to do it again. That's why they might have to do my foot again in a couple of months, because I've had to have special boots made at the moment because one of them isn't quite right. They're waiting for the other operation to settle down first. They're just trying really now to hope that it

corrects my balance. Because once my balance is solved there's not must else, you know... I didn't have that good a balance before. It was fifty-fifty. And if this operation doesn't work they might have to do something to my ear. Maybe that would help, I don't really know. They just have little stabs at it and see what happens.

These descriptions of operations and spells in hospital illustrate some of the acute episodes associated with disability. Nevertheless they comprise only a partial picture of the meaning of physical disability, which is typically a persistent and chronic condition.

Consequences of personal disability

The ways in which pupils spontaneously mentioned they were handicapped by their disabilities were many and various. Occasionally they explained how their disability affected them in almost every possible way, as in the case of the girl who very poignantly said

It (my disability) stops me from doing what I want to do. You know if I feel like taking up games and running around I can't do it... Lots of things. You know, just having the urge to do something and not being able to do it. Maybe climbing up the ladder onto the roof—I can't do it. I can't go swimming because I'll get too cold and I'll get pains. Wear maybe a flimsy top, I can't, I've got to constantly stuff myself with clothes and jumpers and coats. Going places—I can't, because you know sometimes places I go, sometimes they don't want someone who's got something wrong with them. Sometimes I want to take up work and sometimes I want a Saturday job. I've been looking ever since the third year for a Saturday job, but I haven't got one. And I don't think I ever will, because people are not willing to take on physically handicapped people. Even if it's a sitting job.

Not all pupils, however, presented such a broad outlook when discussing consequences of disability. In general, responses conformed to one of several patterns and so, for ease of presentation of the data, subjects are classified according to whether they mentioned outcomes that are principally physical, that mainly affect going out and mixing with friends, that essentially reflect stigma or that refer to more general other worries. Pupils are rated on whether or not they cited each of these four types of consequence of disability, and patterns of responses shown by the sample are presented in Table 9. The most striking finding is that members of all three groups of disabled pupils—the juniors and the seniors in special education, and the seniors in integrated education—were much more likely to note physical, than other, consequences of disability.

Of the numerous children to emphasize physical limitations, a nine year-old girl with a hole-in-the-heart said

I can't run about a lot, I get out of breath, and things like that.

and a boy of the same age with spina bifida observed

Well I can only run for a little while, then my leg kind of flops.

Other pupils mentioned problems with dressing, getting into the bath, going up and down stairs, moving around the house, opening doors, walking at all or walking any distance, bending down, putting arms up, running, getting tired quickly, playing football, climbing, swimming, holding things and picking them up, doing up zips and buttons, skipping, falling over, speech, bouncing a basketball, crossing roads, reaching things from cupboards and, in the case of one boy, hitting his brother (!) Often the children tended to name one restriction which seemed to bother them most, although in other instances a variety of limitations were listed. A senior special school pupil with cerebral palsy cited multiple difficulties which included

> Running and talking to people. But if I talk slowly and think about it then I'm okay. But I tend to hurry up, but I'm getting myself to think before I speak so that it comes out clearer I hope... My balance. Sometimes I can go down quite easily but other times a hurricane can come over me...it depends how I feel. If I don't feel very well then I'm down every five minutes it seems... I've got to be careful of my bones. I haven't got brittle bones, it's just that they hurt quite a bit if I hit them.

On the whole the comments made by pupils in the three groups were similar, the main difference between those of the integrated pupils and the rest lying in the length of answers given. A boy at the comprehensive school, who was confined to a wheelchair by spina bifida, elaborated more fully than some of the others on what he would like to do but could not:

> I'd like to run about and climb trees and what have you. You know, like a typical boy would do. I would like to do all that, and run about. That's one thing I would like to do. I can get out of the chair and crawl around and—it depends how high the tree is—I can climb a tree. You know, with a rope, get up the rope like. The problem is getting down the tree. My brother has to come and catch me sometimes. Or have a trampoline at the bottom and dive off the tree onto the trampoline.

Even if children are sometimes helped with certain tasks, it is clear that a few would be able to achieve a greater level of independence with more encouragement and determination. This was a point made forcefully by a girl of fifteen with spina bifida in normal education who, in commenting about getting dressed, said

> My dad used to do it up to when I was about 12 when one day I said 'No, I've got fed up with this. I'll do it myself now.' So he stood and watched me do it, then he let me do it on my own.

The same pupil went on to say

> 'Cos up to the time I was 12 my mum was washing my hair and ironing my clothes. Then one day I thought 'This is a bit stupid, she can't do it all my life so I might as well do it myself.' So one day she went out, and when she came back I'd ironed all the clothes and she said 'Cor, you're getting good.'

Eleven subjects in the sample as a whole specifically said that their physical disability was detrimental to their social life, as it affected both getting around and making friends. Half of these were, as shown in Table 9, the comprehensive pupils. A similar proportion overall admitted that they felt stigmatized in some way, and again these were most likely to be the disabled integrated seniors.

Teasing and other unkind behaviour is discussed further later. At this point, however, it is worth stressing that the observation of a nine year-old—'No-one's ever said anything nasty to me'—was not typical. Some children experienced severe frustration in having to endure not only their physical limitations but also personal insult. One pupil was particularly affected in this way, remarking

> I don't get on with people because they call me all sorts of names. I think it's the names that most hurt you being handicapped. That's what did me first.

Apparently she was sometimes called 'spastic' (although her condition was in fact spina bifida) and stared at by passers-by in the street. A prime target for teasing at school was her special boots:

> They see the boots and they start calling you names. They call me 'Dr. Marten's' and 'gum boots', things like that, and I don't find it funny.

Her case was not isolated, and it did seem that some children felt quite overwhelmed by the labels and treatment they were fairly regularly subjected to.

Worries of some kind or another seemed to be a very real and direct consequence of disability for a number of children, especially those in the older groups. Almost half of the integrated pupils, and almost a third of the seniors in special education, cited this type of outcome (see Table 9).

Certain kinds of worries have already been hinted at in this chapter. For instance some children were worried about what had caused their disability, about their inability to go out and make friends, or about the social rejection they experienced. Here we consider other kinds of worries, some of them rather general and others considerably more specific. In examining these it is useful to bear in mind what is probably a valid point that was made by one 15 year-old pupil who was asked if she ever got worried because of her disability:

> Of course. I'm sure all handicapped children get worried now and again. I just wonder why it happened, how it happened. It's not on my mind all the time, but I do think about it now and again.

Nevertheless some children appeared realistically to have come to terms with their disabilities—although this did not imply that they never worried. For instance a pupil in a wheelchair commented

> It worries me once or twice, you know. I *do* get depressed sometimes and my mum gets me out of my depression... I've been to see a psychiatrist and it's just ways to get me feeling sorry for myself. It's not worth it, you know. I'm not allowed to think about myself, you know.

Likewise an eight year-old told us

> I have to keep my spirits up. I do sometimes get tired but I have to keep my spirits up a lot. That's the only way to win.

Quite a number of children, furthermore, put on a very brave face and said how lucky they really were. The boy above, who had rejected psychiatric help, and who was considerably disabled himself, volunteered

> I feel sorry for some of these *severely* handicapped, one who's probably got stiff arms and legs and I think is called spastic. I wouldn't like to be in his or her state. I'm happy to be the way that I am.

Much the same sentiment was expressed by another pupil who had cerebral palsy (spasticity) and who claimed

Characteristics of group	Physical Aspects				Mixing/Getting Out				Stigma				Worries/Other			
	Not mentioned		Mentioned		Not mentioned		Mentioned		Not mentioned		Mentioned		Not mentioned		Mentioned	
	No.	% of group	No.	% of group	No.	% of group	No.	% of group	No.	% of group	No.	% of group	No.	% of group	No.	% of group
Juniors in special education (N=29)	4	13.8	25	86.2	27	93.1	2	6.9	24	82.8	5	17.2	26	89.7	3	10.3
Seniors in special education (N=17)	1	5.9	16	94.1	14	82.4	3	17.6	16	94.1	1	5.9	12	70.6	5	29.4
Seniors in integrated education (N=13)	2	15.4	11	84.6	7	53.8	6	46.2	8	61.5	5	38.5	7	53.8	6	46.2
TOTAL	7	11.9	52	88.1	48	81.4	11	18.6	48	81.4	11	18.6	45	76.3	14	23.7

Table 9: Consequences of personal disability spontaneously mentioned by physically disabled pupils

38

Well I think, so what, I am handicapped, so why bother about it? There's always other people worse off than me so I think that I'm lucky to be how I am and what I am and what for. So I think, so what, who cares? Not me.

The way that many, especially the older, children seemed to have come to terms with their disability was impressive. So often the question of 'what, anyway, is normality?' was raised, many subjects taking the line of a 14 year-old with muscular dystrophy who maintained

I try and be normal. I try and do, to what extent I can, things that are normal.

Not all children, however, were well able to cope with their frustrations, and several admitted to quite serious worries. A 13 year-old girl whose disability stemmed from polio reported

I do (worry) quite a lot. I wish I was like everyone else. There's no difference in me, but I wish I could be like everyone else. Then they won't leave me out and lots of things.

In two other cases children specifically mentioned what were probably realistic worries concerning valves fitted for spina bifida with hydrocephalus. One of these was concerned that, because of his lack of feeling, his valve might go wrong without his knowing about it. A rather different, but equally understandable, worry was pointed out by a 15 year-old girl with spina bifida who appeared to have had no kind, however informal, of genetic counselling. Indeed we noted the desire of many disabled children for more information about their physical condition and its prognosis.

Summary
Just over half the able-bodied juniors, and all the able-bodied seniors, mentioned disabled acquaintances. Most of these pupils could describe the impairments of the people they named, although only a minority could provide clinical diagnoses. Several disabled pupils also had a limited understanding of disability. Considerably less than half of those in special education were able to give a personal diagnosis, and less than a third had any idea of the cause of their own impairment. Indeed only among the disabled seniors in ordinary education could the majority of pupils name their physical condition and give some indication of its origin.

On the whole it appeared that opportunities for discussion of disability were infrequent for the children we spoke to. Only a small minority of the disabled pupils indicated that the topic was ever raised with parents, siblings and professionals.

Disabled pupils most often mentioned physical limitations when discussing the main consequences of their impairments, and only a small proportion cited other outcomes such as effects on social life and worries in general. Nevertheless, some pupils may well have been handicapped by their impairments in ways not referred to during the interviews, just as those who mentioned limitations indicated that their importance varied in intensity. This was particularly evident from the comments made about worries, and many of the pupils who did admit to occasional worries also appeared remarkably well adjusted to their physical state.

4 The question of education

In this chapter we present pupils' views on education. First we examine the school satisfaction expressed by all pupils, some of whom have experienced both special and ordinary education, and then we ask whether pupils would prefer to go to other schools, including boarding schools. Lastly, and importantly, we explore in considerable detail the opinions of both disabled and non-disabled children on the advantages and disadvantages of special and ordinary education for pupils with physical impairments.

School satisfaction

One of the first questions we asked pupils was what they thought of their own current school. As shown in Table 10, many more children could think of reasons why they *did* like their school than why they *did not*, although four in ten made both favourable and unfavourable comments.

Interestingly, there was no straightforward way in which school satisfaction seemed related to age, disability or school. Nevertheless it is worth noting that, generally speaking, the physically disabled pupils in special education were less critical of their schooling than were their peers in the integrated provisions. All the same, numbers are small and the disabled children placed in the comprehensive schools may well not only have been more intellectually able, and therefore possibly more critical, but they are also more likely to have had more different schooling experiences. For such reasons response rates are probably of less significance than the comments voiced by individual pupils.

Turning to these comments, it seemed that children from all groups tended to give the same kinds of reasons for liking or not liking their school. The lessons, getting into trouble, too much hard work (or too much easy work), the other children, the teachers, sports, outings, facilities and school dinners were most often mentioned in support of likes and dislikes. To give some examples, a satisfied nine year-old at the ordinary primary school said he was happy where he was because

> You can play football with balls, and when you can't do your work the teacher helps you. And in maths when we can't do it we ask Sir if he can look it up in his book and see if he can show us how to do it, and he shows us.

An equally happy 11 year-old girl from the same school reported that

Characteristics of group	Advantages only mentioned		Disadvantages only mentioned		Advantages and disadvantages mentioned		Not known		Total
	No.	% of group	No.	% of group	No.	% of group	No.	% of group	No.
Able-bodied									
Juniors	6	37.5	—	—	10	62.5	—	—	16
Seniors	9	69.2	—	—	4	30.8	—	—	13
Physically disabled									
Juniors in special education	15	51.7	3	10.3	8	27.6	3	10.3	29
Seniors in special education	9	52.9	1	5.9	7	36.8	—	—	17
Seniors in integrated education	5	38.5	1	7.7	7	53.8	—	—	13
Total	44	50	5	5.7	36	40.9	3	3.4	88

Table 10: Satisfaction with schooling

41

> It's a nice school and it's got good rules—not to run and that, not to do naughty things, no fighting. That's the sort of thing I like about it. And there's good work, and we can go swimming and do sports.

On the other hand some of the other pupils at this school felt there were grounds for complaint. One ten year-old told us

> I don't like some of the teachers. Because Miss —— , she gets in a temper a lot. When she gets in a temper she walks up to us and takes us out to the headmaster. And then we don't like it because we get into trouble.

while a younger girl commented

> I don't like some of the work we have to do—it's too easy.

The older non-disabled children at the comprehensive schools said much the same kinds of things, although they were generally less verbose. As one 15 year-old girl put it

> It's alright. I enjoy doing sports and things like that. It's just like any other school really, isn't it?

Indeed 'it's alright' was a typical response, and only four of this group of 13 mentioned any dislikes at all. These four cited having to get to school too early, not strict enough teachers and a dislike of some of the other children.

Perhaps the expressions of greatest enthusiasm for their schools came from special school pupils.

> I like the school dinners—mmm. I like the teachers and also I like the headmistress. There's nothing I don't like.

said a nine year-old with spina bifida, and an eight year-old said her school was

> Very, very nice... There's a swimming pool and there's a big playground and, well, I've got lots of friends.

Nevertheless some children were more tempered in their comments, such as the cerebral palsied 11 year-old who told us

> It's not bad. They're not too strict and they don't give you too hard work. When we go on outings... pop concerts... and see people who are alive...I like that especially if I like him.

All the same some special school pupils could raise no comments in favour of their placements. Several mentioned lessons they did not like whereas others were less explicit about their dislikes. Most vociferous, however, was probably the ten year-old boy with spina bifida who said

> Yes, I am being honest and I absolutely hate it here... because, for one thing, I get beaten up, and also because when you go out to play it is never for long.

Interestingly, however, none of the pupils citing disadvantages made comments that could be said to relate directly to the fact that they attended a special school. This is in marked contrast to the responses given by the physically disabled pupils integrated into local comprehensive schools, who tended to take the question about whether or not they liked their school as a cue for comparing it with the special school they had previously attended. Some of their comments on this question are presented in the following section.

Transfer from special to ordinary education
Thirteen pupils in our sample were former pupils of the borough special school but currently attenders at nearby comprehensive schools. Their comments on school likes and dislikes could—and often spontaneously did—therefore draw on personal experience of both special and integrated provisions.

The youngest disabled pupil at a comprehensive school was an 11 year-old girl with spina bifida. She had only recently changed schools and said

> I like this school better than Lime School* because I can play with the ordinary friends. You can mix with my other friends in the class.

She added

> You get much harder work here than when you were at Lime School. You know it's much harder and it's better. It's good work, and good lessons, nice teachers—they're all nice.

For a 14 year-old boy with muscular dystrophy, the main outcome of the transfer was, as he saw it, that

> I feel a bit more independent than at the other school... There's not always someone looking after you here—you're a bit more free to do what you want... I didn't *hate* it at the other school. I liked it. But there were physios, doctors and that. Here you feel a bit more normal I suppose.

The advantages of feeling more 'normal' were also stressed by a 15 year-old pupil confined to a wheelchair. In his words the merits of ordinary education are that

> You've got more opportunities—jobs and education-wise. At the Lime School all they teach you is just basics. You've got a chance to go to a higher level here. You learn to live with normal people—when you're at a special school you're surrounded by handicapped kids. When you're at normal school you learn how to live with normal people and make friends with them.
> At this one, you see different teachers, everything... it's different. I just want to mix for a change. When I move in a handicapped school I really *feel* handicapped. When I've been in a normal school I feel like I'm like the rest of them. Just like counting myself like them.
> I just want to be mixed. 'Cos when I used to be in Lime School I though 'Oh God, would I ever go to a normal school?' I thought I was really handicapped, but now I'm here and mixed and it's fun.

Another 15 year-old was similarly glad he had taken part in the integration scheme:

> You learn more and when you're at Lime School you missed a lot of the lessons for having physio, and sometimes you could miss anything up to half a lesson. And, well here, you have physio at dinner time and the work is what the other kids are doing. When you were at Lime School the work wasn't the same. You didn't stand so much chance of going to college as I

*Lime School is used throughout as a pseudonym for the name of the special school.

did when I came here. That's the main thing.

He added

> Well I can make more friends... when I'm here. There's more people, mainly.

and

> Well you get a bit more freedom at breaktimes and dinnertimes. At Lime School you had to go into the dining hall at a set time and finish all together. You know, when you'd finished dinner you had to wait for everybody else and you missed a lot of the lunch hour. Here you can go into your dinner, you have to line up, but you can go as soon as you're finished.

Nevertheless not all integrated pupils had only positive comments to make. A 13 year-old boy, for instance, did not like

> People teasing me. Boys, you know, copy the way I walk, and the teachers shout at me when I don't do nothing. Say somebody done something, she (the teacher) caught me sort of looking. She think I done it, but I never. I sort of shout and lose my temper, and sort of swear and stuff like that. I don't mean to do it, it's just that they don't understand.

Another pupil to comment on this issue was a 14 year-old boy with spina bifida. In his view

> There are a few things I don't like, otherwise I like it here... I just like the education and the teachers and the long dinner times—it's quite good.
> I try to get friends but sometimes they just don't want to know. So it's a bit hard making friends—it's got slightly easier, but not very much.

Finally, it is worth quoting the comments of one of the oldest pupils in the sample who said of her comprehensive school:

> Well I wouldn't say I *like* it, but then I don't *hate* it... The things I like about it is that you've got a chance to express the way you feel... you've got the chance to do what you like. Like at Lime School, the games and your friends, they're just like you—handicapped... you've got more range of lessons. At Lime School you are sort of taught maths, English, cookery. But here you've got French, all the different languages, Greek... things like that... It's harder work. Because at Lime School I sort of took it for granted that that's what we'd be doing here, you know sort of easy work... and I thought that if I was a good girl and studied my books—well, I'd get a good job at the end of it. Now I'm here I'm realising that it's a bit different. You've got to really study more, and lots of things you've got to know. At Lime School they just sort of taught you—I didn't think you'd ever need to know more, until I was here.

Despite the clear fact that most of the physically disabled children integrated into local ordinary secondary schools were glad, on balance, to have left the special school, many did relate problems they had had in settling into their new school.

A 15 year-old girl with cerebral palsy, for instance, noted that the transition had not been smooth for her:

> It was pretty difficult when we first came here, you know straight into first year, because we were the first people to actually go down into the other building and start coming from scratch. But now, apart from all the new people who are coming in, who sort of say 'oooh, that's strange' you know, but everybody in my year, 3rd year you know, they've got so used to it that

it's just treated as 'well hello, you're a pupil.'

Similarly a boy of the same age, but who had muscular dystrophy, described how the first six months in the comprehensive school had been the hardest time for him:

> Well I didn't want to come, at that time. Because it was new to me and, well once I got here, the first half of the year was the hardest time, trying to mix in with others, because when you're at Lime School you lose touch with people. When you come to a school like this you've got, I mean you get, an attitude where you think people should feel sorry for you and things like that. But now, after I've been here a few years, I'm just like one of the other pupils.

He went on to explain how the differences between the two schools made the changeover particularly stressful:

> When you're at Lime School and you do things, they don't care. When you come to this school, like you go to eat your dinner, right, you have to struggle a lot. Everyone can see you, and instead of not taking any notice of it, they look at you. Then you start thinking 'why should they look at me?' Then you start thinking 'they don't feel sorry for me, in that way'. Or they look at you, maybe they do feel sorry for you, but it makes you feel a bit, well a bit embarrassed, things like that. Then you start thinking about what's wrong with you. But that's only, for me it was only about six months, and then it was alright.

Several other pupils made similar kinds of points, and said how they had been teased when they first came to the comprehensive school, or how they had been overwhelmed by such large numbers of active children around them all the time. Nevertheless by the time of interview most children felt pretty well settled in their schools, and indeed some understandably resented the links they had to maintain with the special school which they felt they had left.

Contacts with the special school were normally only for physiotherapy, medicals and swimming. However industrial action on the part of lunch supervisors at the time we spoke to the children meant that the ex-special school pupils were having to return to their old school for lunch rather than being allowed to fend for themselves locally with their non-disabled friends and peers. Evidently this was not a popular practice from our respondents' point-of-view. Nevertheless they tended to be philosophical about the matter, one 14 year-old girl saying that when you go back to the old school

> You do feel a bit funny, but it's alright because you know you're one of them.

All the same this particular pupil did feel rather bitter about the restrictions imposed upon the disabled pupils:

> That's the reason I don't really like it. Because whenever you want to do something you can't because the Lime School stops us... Well, like you want to go home with your friends, you know after school, like I usually do—you can't. Like if you need a note and you forget it, you can't go... And, you know, they just don't let you do things. Like now, when I wanted to go out to dinner with my friends, they wouldn't let me go. Because they said if anything happens it's their responsibility. But if you bring a note it's not their responsibility because it's our parents. It's them that's allowed us to go. Before they used to say if you bring a note you're allowed to do what you want, but now they're saying you can't, even if you bring a note.

Overall, then, children transferred from special to ordinary schools were realistic about the problems such a move could bring, although most felt that the advantages of their new situation outweighed the disadvantages. A representative summary comment was provided by a 15 year-old girl with cerebral palsy who said

They say you've broken away from it, but you've not.

but added

It's no real ties, it's fine.

Preferences for other schools

Related to likes and dislikes of present schools are wishes to be placed elsewhere. Children's opinions on this question are shown in Table 11. They demonstrate quite clearly that it was those in the special school who were most likely to say they would prefer to attend a different school (even though, as a group, they were most appreciative of their current placements) and that it was those at the comprehensives who appeared to be most happy to stay where they were.

Of the children in ordinary schools, then, most were content to remain where they were. Nevertheless four ordinary junior school pupils said they would prefer to be elsewhere—they either wanted to return to schools they had previously attended or, in the case of one child, wanted to go to school in Cyprus—and one physically disabled pupil in a comprehensive school wanted to return to special education as he could see no advantages of integration.

It is the responses of the children in special education, however, which are of most interest. Overall 39 per cent of these pupils clearly

Characteristics of group	Would not prefer other school		Would prefer other school		Not known		Total
	No.	% of group	No.	% of group	No.	% of group	No.
Able-bodied							
Juniors	12	75	4	25	—	—	16
Seniors	11	84.6	—	—	2	15.4	13
Physically disabled							
Juniors in special education	16	55.2	11	37.9	2	6.9	29
Seniors in special education	6	35.3	7	41.2	4	23.5	17
Seniors in integrated education	10	76.9	1	7.7	2	15.4	13
Total	55	62.5	23	26.1	10	11.4	88

Table 11: School preferences

indicated that they would rather be at other schools. Various reasons were given, such as not wanting to travel so far to school, disliking having to journey by coach, or missing friends from previous schools.

Besides these sorts of general reasons for wishing to change schools, a considerable number of 'special' pupils did specifically say they would prefer to go to an ordinary school.

> I would like to see what happens there in a normal school.

said one nine year-old, while an eight year-old commented that in ordinary schools

> You could go out with the schools much more often and meet new friends.

Indeed quite a few children thought they would make more friends at a normal school. Others felt you could have 'more fun', 'speak different languages', 'wear a uniform' and 'get to go out to the shops during your break and get to go out with your friends a lot more during the school time'. Of course it is difficult to know how strongly most children felt about their expressed wishes to change schools, but one nine year-old boy with cerebral palsy did seem to put his case particularly convincingly. In his words

> I would like to change schools and not a handicapped school. I want to go somewhere where there's no handicapped children... I hate handicap... They make me angry.

His demands stretched to a school

> Where there's all boys—no girls.

To place these comments in context it should be stressed that some children seemed very happy at the special school, such as the seven year-old cerebral palsied girl who, when asked if she would prefer to go to another school, said

> No, I like this too well best.

And others, while recognising the possibilities of ordinary schools, still thought that they were best placed where they were. A nine year-old, for example, reported that

> My mother wants me here until I'm 16. This is a handicapped school and I'm handicapped as well.

and a 12 year-old said that she would like to go to an ordinary school, although she added simply

> But I just can't.

Thoughts on residential schools

We asked all the children whether they had ever thought that they would like to go to a boarding school, and who they believed usually went to this kind of school. Very few children expressed any desire to go away to school, but older pupils had clearly given the greatest thought to the general question of residential education. Disabled children were most likely to have friends at boarding schools.

Two-thirds of the able-bodied juniors were hostile to the idea of attending a boarding school, and either simply stated that they preferred to remain at home, or apparently saw removal from home as a punishment. One boy told us that children were sent away to school

> Because they do naughty things like keep swearing at their mum and things... my mum told me.

Among the rest, however, two children described positive aspects of life at a residential school. An eight year-old girl thought that she would enjoy it and said

> I think it's fun, because I like it because—is it a kind of house with bunk beds? I like sleeping on the top of the bed.

while a slightly older boy hoped to go away to school because

> I'll learn more... and it's easier to get a job.

The remaining two children in this group appeared to have neutral feelings about boarding school education: they described circumstances in which it might be helpful, but they did not indicate that they would like to go to such a school themselves.

A fairly similar pattern of responses was given by the disabled juniors in special education. Two-thirds of these pupils definitely did not want to go to a boarding school, and indeed one eight year-old boy was most adamant on this score:

> I'd hate going there—sleep there, wash there!

A further one in five of the pupils seemed unable to answer our question, and two children were undecided.

None of the able-bodied seniors wanted to go away to school themselves, but they were much more aware than the juniors of the varied circumstances that might lead to a child's attendance at a boarding school, and a quarter mentioned possible benefits of an education away from home. A 16 year-old girl commented that

> The education authorities might think that a boarding school has more to offer them (children with special needs) than a school like this.

A further one in four of these pupils felt that children at boarding schools had often been rejected by their parents. An 11 year-old girl explained that children went away to school

> Because they're naughty sometimes... 'Cos their mums don't want them and they go away... and they go to boarding schools.

The remaining pupils had less clear views, or perhaps saw more than one side to the question. A 13 year-old boy, for instance, replied in some detail, carefully weighing strong personal disadvantages against the possible advantages:

> I don't think I'd like to go to a boarding school, because the first reason is I like to have a room of my own and I wouldn't like to sleep in a big dormitory kind of thing with lots of other boys. The second reason is that I am at the mercy of my hobby [he makes models]—I wouldn't like to see them break things... I wouldn't like boarding school. I want to see my mum and other members of my family. It might make me a bit more independent though. I don't know, never having been to boarding school.

Seven of the 13 disabled seniors at the comprehensive schools mentioned that a parent or doctor had suggested to them that they might like to go, as one boy put it, 'into residential', and several more talked of friends at boarding schools. This is in sharp contrast to the situation of the able-bodied seniors, none of whom said they had discussed such a possibility or appeared to know anyone at a boarding school.

Four disabled pupils in the integration scheme commented on educational advantages stemming from a residential school education, and one girl elaborated upon these. She thought that there were

All sorts of advantages associated with it. I used to have to miss a lot of school because of my illness, so I think that in a boarding school probably they'll have a doctor or a nurse there and still yet I'll be at school and I can study there... I wouldn't miss so much work as I miss here, because I have to go away for a month, two months sometimes.

However, more than half the integrated pupils believed that some children attended boarding schools because of family problems. A 13 year-old girl explained that this happened

'Cos their mothers can't cope and they get more pleasure there.

Certainly a residential placement seemed to have been considered for the 15 year-old boy who told us:

My mum keeps on saying to me that when I was born—you know, the people who deliver you—they said that they should put me in a school straight away, so I'd grow up there. She keeps on saying that she wished she did this instead of keeping me. So I just get fed up and say I wish I was there. I wouldn't be happy not knowing my brothers and sisters, my mum and my dad, but I would have been happier in a way that I was not sort of out and about. Because in a boarding school you're not very free to do what you want... I think she (my mum) only says it when she gets angry—she don't mean it.

Some of these pupils were vehemently opposed to boarding school education. As one girl said, 'I just want to be mixed.' Another senior added:

I think it's terrible, people who do that. You just feel they don't want them no more, they get fed up with them. But I would never do that, send any of them to a boarding school. I couldn't. Even though some of the other children are worse than me... I wouldn't care how they are, I'd still keep them you know, look after them. It's just that some people are just like it. My mum would never do it.

These pupils were evidently equating boarding schools with residential education for the physically disabled.

The strength of feeling expressed by the integrated seniors both for and against residential schools surprised us. Some pupils saw advantages in educational terms to be gained from this type of schooling, while others interpreted being 'sent away' as a form of rejection. Nevertheless only two disabled pupils clearly indicated that they wanted to go away to school themselves. A 15 year-old boy's conclusions touched on the complexity of the matter:

I think it really depends on the person... If the person is the kind of person who would like it, then they should be allowed to go. They should have the choice. Of course.

The disabled seniors at the special school did not seem to have given the subject of residential schools the same amount of thought as their integrated peers. Only one pupil expressed any interest in going to such a school, and only one pupil mentioned that he had discussed the matter with his mother.

Special versus ordinary education
All the young people we talked to, whether they attended special or ordinary schools, and whether or not they were disabled themselves, were asked for their views on the advantages and disadvantages of different kinds of schooling for children with physical impairments.

Table 12 shows that the likelihood that pupils would mention advantages of special schools and advantages of integrated provision is greater among some groups than others. It was the junior pupils at the ordinary primary school and the senior pupils at the special school who were most likely to cite the merits of segregation, and the senior pupils—both disabled and able-bodied—at the comprehensive schools who were least likely to. Most of these latter groups did not, however, see only advantages of mixed schooling. Rather they tended to see both advantages and disadvantages of each kind of provision.

The young disabled children at the special school did not conform to any general pattern of response. Over four in ten could not understand the question well enough, or did not have sufficiently clear opinions on the matter, to be able to cite advantages or disadvantages. Of the rest, there was a fairly even three-way split between those who claimed only advantages, only disadvantages, or a more balanced view.

Advantages of special education
Advantages of special education mentioned by the children fell into four main categories. These are that special schooling provides opportunities for more individual attention, that it protects pupils from undue teasing and curiosity, that it aids an acceptance of personal disability and that it caters best for the physical needs of children with impairments. Responses that did not easily fit under any of these heads were included within an 'other benefit' category.

When pupils' comments on the positive aspects of special schooling are examined in this way (see Table 13) it is found that, overall, more children mentioned extra individual attention than any other benefit—although this was noted by only about a third of the sample. Less than one in five pupils mentioned physical reasons and protection from teasing as advantages of segregated provision, and only one in eleven thought that the handicapped would find it easier to come to terms with their disability if they mixed only with other disabled children.

This general picture, however, obscures the contrasting patterns of responses provided by the different groups of pupils. The ordinary junior school pupils, for example, were marginally most likely to cite less curiosity and teasing as an advantage of special education, and they were equally likely to mention 'more individual attention' and less physical problems as additional benefits. Nevertheless it was a minority of children who cited advantages falling into any of the categories.

Characteristics of group	Advantages of special education only mentioned		Advantages of ordinary education only mentioned		Advantages of special & ordinary education mentioned		Not known/ Did not understand		Total
	No.	% of group	No.	% of group	No.	% of group	No.	% of group	No.
Able-bodied									
Juniors	9	56.3	2	12.5	3	18.8	2	12.5	16
Seniors	3	23.1	1	7.7	9	69.2	—	—	13
Physically disabled									
Juniors in special education	6	20.7	5	17.2	6	20.7	12	41.4	29
Seniors in special education	9	52.9	1	5.9	4	23.5	3	17.6	17
Seniors in integrated education	1	7.7	—	—	12	92.3	—	—	13
Total	28	31.8	9	10.2	34	38.6	17	19.3	88

Table 12: Advantages of special and ordinary education for the disabled

Spontaneous comments from this group further illuminate the quantitative data. Thus a ten year-old boy volunteered the opinion that 'nothing could be better in an ordinary school' and proceeded to tell a rather ambiguous story of a disabled girl who had gone to an ordinary school and died. Another somewhat confused explanation (obviously generalizing from blindness) of the merits of special education for disabled children was given by a nine year-old boy who felt that in an ordinary school

> The teacher wouldn't understand them and they don't do work like we do. They've got this piece of paper and they've all got dots on it and they can tell what it says.

Other children, however, responded by raising conventional arguments in favour of special education for the disabled. Some stressed that special schools have more staff which both helps learning and means that children can more easily be accompanied around the school. Yet others mentioned the needs of some children for special equipment which is not provided in ordinary schools.

As already shown, slightly more of this group of children mentioned the likelihood of less teasing and name-calling than noted any other possible benefit of special education. By way of illustration, an eight year-old commented

> I think they'd be better in a special school. Because when you're in an ordinary school other people, they make fun of you. Because handicapped people are handicapped. So they make fun of you.

and an 11 year-old said

> The best thing for them is to stay in another school, so they won't feel sorry for themselves—not to see other people, because they can't do the same things. They could come to a school like this and be in one class, but if there's another school...

One in three of the children interviewed from the special schools—especially the younger pupils—did not or could not list the merits and demerits of different forms of schooling for the disabled. Of those who did proffer an opinion, however, there was a marked difference in the frequency with which advantages falling in the different categories were mentioned: ten children cited extra individual attention as an advantage of special education and ten gave reasons which most easily fitted the 'other' category, whereas only one said that segregation could help pupils accept their disabilities. Four children thought there would be less curiosity and teasing in special schools, and four felt there would be less physical problems.

Many of these children were quite brief in their comments, although what they did say tended to mirror what the other groups of pupils said. Thus children said things such as 'There's more space and no stairs' at special schools, 'At our school the staff help you' and that you have opportunities to do 'exercises'. At greater length a 14 year-old girl expressed her appreciation of special education when she said

> You can learn better. You've got more attention from the teachers. When I used to go to the other school they used to call me 'handicapped', 'bandy legs' and things like that because of the way I walked. I don't walk straight.

Characteristics of group	More individual attention				Less curiosity & teasing				Aids acceptance of handicap				Easier for physical reasons				Other			
	Not Mentioned		Mentioned		Not Mentioned		Mentioned		Not Mentioned		Mentioned		Not Mentioned		Mentioned		Not Mentioned		Mentioned	
	No.	% of group	No.	% of group	No.	% of group	No.	% of group	No.	% of group	No.	% of group	No.	% of group	No.	% of group	No.	% of group	No.	% of group
Able-bodied																				
Juniors	12	75	4	25	11	68.8	5	31.3	13	81.3	3	18.8	12	75	4	25	14	87.5	2	12.5
Seniors	6	46.2	7	53.8	11	84.6	2	15.4	11	84.6	2	15.4	11	84.6	2	15.4	11	84.6	2	15.4
Physically disabled																				
Juniors in special education	24	82.8	5	17.2	27	93.1	2	6.9	28	96.6	1	3.4	28	96.6	1	3.4	25	86.2	4	13.8
Seniors in special education	12	70.6	5	29.4	15	88.2	2	11.8	17	100	—	—	14	82.4	3	17.6	11	64.7	6	35.3
Seniors in integrated education	6	46.2	7	53.8	9	69.2	4	30.8	11	84.6	2	15.4	7	53.8	6	46.2	13	100	—	—
Total	60	68.2	28	31.8	73	83	15	17	80	90.9	8	9.1	72	81.8	16	18.2	74	84.1	14	15.9

Table 13: Advantages of special schools mentioned

More of this group than any other, however, gave reasons favouring special education which did not fall within the four main categories described above. For instance being let off work 'if we don't want to do it', the comment that 'at a normal school most of the teachers just take the mickey out of you' and more holidays and trips were among the additional reasons children gave for feeling that special education is advantageous for the disabled.

Turning next to the secondary school able-bodied pupils, all but one could think of advantages of special provision for the disabled, even if they could also list disadvantages. Overwhelmingly they were most likely to mention the extra individual attention possible in special education.

Some of these pupils, however, distinguished *between* categories of disability, particularly when considering possibilities of integration within their own school. In this way a 17 year-old girl, who was generally favourable to mixed schooling, did say in relation to special schools that

> I think they're best for really handicapped children who couldn't cope with a normal school like this. Because there's a lot of energy in this school—a lot of children have got a lot of energy.

As on other questions, it was the senior disabled pupils in the integration scheme who had the most to say. Every single member of this group mentioned advantages of special education—although all but one also mentioned disadvantages. Many of the comments made by these pupils were personal, and some have already been presented. Others, however, were more general and a nearer match to those made by the other pupil groups.

Over half of these older disabled pupils stressed the extra individual attention possible in special schools. For example one girl said that

> Because most special schools tend to be smaller than the average school, I suppose teachers will come round and explain what they're talking about in detail. Because there were about 80 or so of us in Lime School. Here, you know, there's double that proportion. I think that's the advantage.

For others, such as a 14 year-old boy who was wheelchair-bound, practical advantages seemed paramount:

> (A special school) is much easier, it's obvious it's much easier. Because you're all handicapped people there, so it's much easier. Easier in getting around, because at this school we've only got three minutes to get from one classroom to another. That's a bit difficult. Because when this (interview) finishes I've got to go to the next lesson which is up there somewhere, up in the lift and then straight across...

Many of these pupils differentiated between disabilities and children, and indicated that whereas most of the disabled could be integrated successfully, there would inevitably be some of the more severely disabled for whom special provisions would be necessary. The view of a 15 year-old with spina bifida was that

> All handicapped kids should start out at a special school, just to see what their abilities are. And if it's possible—if they're good enough— then go to a normal school. But obviously for some kids it's impossible for them to go to a normal school, so they'll have to stay at a special school... At a place like

this there's stairs to manage. If you can't manage the stairs, you're done. You've got to get upstairs for lessons. And also you've got to keep up.

In other words these children who were in ordinary schools despite their disabilities did nonetheless recognise that there could be advantages of special education in specific cases. Several emphasized the need for choice by individual children, particularly as both gains and losses were involved whichever type of school was selected. This was explicitly recognised by one pupil who said of the physically disabled:

> In some cases they're better at a handicapped school, because say you get someone with spina bifida, they've got to learn to walk. They come to a school like this and most of the time is in lessons. And then you've got to work out what's more important, someone walking or having better knowledge. It's like that.

Advantages of ordinary education

Three main ways in which physically disabled children might benefit from integrated schooling were mentioned by the pupils. These are a greater opportunity to mix with other children, more 'normal' experiences and education of a higher academic standard. The frequency with which children in the sample mentioned these possible advantages—or indeed cited any other benefit—are shown in Table 14.

Interestingly, each of the three main types of advantages were noted by about the same number of children: each was claimed to be important by approximately one in five of the respondents. Nevertheless, as before, patterns of answers were rather different within the separate sub-groups of children.

The non-disabled junior pupils in ordinary education, who had no disabled children at their school, apparently saw very few advantages of integration. Only one child said that ordinary schooling meant opportunities for greater social mix for the disabled and only three mentioned other ways in which ordinary schooling could promote normalization. Furthermore, none of these pupils seemed aware of the possibility of varying academic emphasis within different types of schools.

So it was atypically that a nine year-old girl ventured the opinion:

> I think they should all mix so they feel more normal ... I think it helps them to think they're more normal, that there isn't so much wrong with them.

Several children, although not mentioning specific advantages of integration, did nonetheless suggest that things would probably run smoothly if the disabled and able-bodied were in schools together. And three volunteered comments to the effect that the physically able pupils could help the disabled 'with their sticks to go places' or push them around in their wheelchairs.

These observations are of particular interest as they give some idea of the initial attitudes that children would be likely to have were disabled pupils to be introduced into their schools. Generally speaking there were few young able-bodied children apparently in favour of integration. In the words of an eight year-old:

This school ain't for handicapped, and when people are handicapped they go to a handicapped school.

Nevertheless it is true to say that the issue was a rather remote one for this group of pupils, and it is encouraging to note signs of potential acceptance of the disabled among many of them. This is especially noteworthy as at least some of these children were likely to be going on to attend one of the two local comprehensive schools with integration schemes—or other schools with disabled pupils—when they pass the primary school stage.

It is interesting to compare their attitudes with those expressed by the secondary school pupils currently at the integrated comprehensives, and it is instructive to note the marked contrast in viewpoints. As can be seen from Table 14, almost half of the older pupils mentioned the greater social mix that normal education could bring, and almost a third cited other outcomes encouraging normalization. Less than one in six of these respondents, however, referred to contrasting academic environments in different types of schools.

Illustrative of the kind of statements made by these children is the claim of a 15 year-old that integration for the disabled is good because

They can sort of mix in with people like us as well. You know, we're sort of all the same really. There's nothing different about them as there is about us. So I suppose they just like to be one of us.

As another pupil put it, ordinary education is best as

They're not going to be in a specially protected school when they grow up. They're not going to be a protected élite. And they've got to learn to fend for themselves. Otherwise they'll go out into the big wide world when they leave these special schools and they won't be able to fend for themselves because they'll be so used to being looked after all the time that they won't really know what's happening.

Similar views were expounded by many of the pupils, and highlighted the genuine understanding they seemed to have of the issues involved. This maturity—especially as compared with that shown by the younger junior school pupils—was no doubt due to a combination of both greater age and personal experience of physical disability. These factors appear to have led them to reasoned and balanced views in which both advantages and disadvantages of different types of schooling for disabled pupils were appreciated.

By contrast the physically disabled special school pupils, in general, had little experience of ordinary education and for many the question of relative merits of different types of schooling appeared not to have arisen: overall about one in three—mostly the junior school children—did not really understand the point about comparison, or at least had no idea as to what they thought about it.

All the same, some children in this group did have opinions on the matter—often, it seemed to us, the older brighter children and those who at some previous date had discussed the possibility of transfer to one of the local comprehensive schools. This was certainly true for a 14 year-old boy with spina bifida who told us

I wanted to go there (to one of the comprehensive schools) when I was 11, but I didn't. I missed the advantage of that.

56

Characteristics of group	Greater social mix				Other aspects of normalization				Better education				Other			
	Not Mentioned No.	% of group	Mentioned No.	% of group	Not Mentioned No.	% of group	Mentioned No.	% of group	Not Mentioned No.	% of group	Mentioned No.	% of group	Not Mentioned No.	% of group	Mentioned No.	% of group
Able-bodied																
Juniors	15	93.8	1	6.3	13	81.3	3	18.8	16	100	—	—	16	100	—	—
Seniors	7	53.8	6	46.2	9	69.2	4	30.8	11	84.6	2	15.4	12	92.3	1	7.7
Physically disabled																
Juniors in special education	27	93.1	2	6.9	27	93.1	2	6.9	27	93.1	2	6.9	24	82.8	5	17.2
Seniors in special education	14	82.4	3	17.6	17	100	—	—	15	88.2	2	11.8	17	100	—	—
Seniors in integrated education	6	46.2	7	53.8	5	38.5	8	61.5	3	23.1	10	76.9	13	100	—	—
Total	69	78.4	19	21.6	71	80.7	17	19.3	72	81.8	16	18.2	82	93.2	6	6.8

Table 14: Advantages of integration mentioned

57

Many other pupils gave reasons why *they* themselves would like to go to an ordinary school (see earlier section on preferences for other schools), and some made more general points. According to an eight year-old, for instance, ordinary education is better as

> It's more quiet and they don't fight ... (also) because they do hard work there.

although it should be noted that this was not the view of a 14 year-old boy who felt

> They learn you more here than in an ordinary school. Maths, for instance. They give you hard ones like multiplications.

A somewhat confused, although rather interesting, comment was made by another pupil who said

> They do more fun in an ordinary school. You can go anywhere you like, but here, well you can go anywhere you like but you have to go out more often and my mother doesn't like that and nor do I. We came to school to learn, not to go out.

In general, however, these special school children did not typically indicate advantages of integration, and most seemed happy where they were. But there were exceptions, and a few children gave quite reasoned explanations of benefits to be derived from integrated schooling.

It remains only to look at the feelings of pupils who have transferred from segregated to integrated provision. As shown in Table 14, this is the group most likely to have mentioned advantages of ordinary education for the disabled—although, as we saw earlier, these children also recognised the benefits that special education could bring. Over three-quarters mentioned the higher academic standards in ordinary education, and considerably more than half stressed the greater variety of friends and the greater opportunities for normalization in ordinary schools.

Many of the comments volunteered by these pupils have been incorporated in the earlier discussion of current schooling: asking them what they thought of their present school had tended to elicit comparisons between their experiences in special and ordinary education. Most of the respondents, however, had plenty to say on this question, and all but one saw benefits of integration.

For most of these pupils, advantages in terms of education, social contacts and participation in the normal community were intertwined. A 17 year-old girl, for example, held the view that

> Coming straight out of Lime School into a job, I think it would be a disaster. It would be better to go to a normal school then, after that, because then you get quite used to all these quarrels and problems of, you know, a different life. You get used to what people will say to you outside because they'll say it to you inside ... I used to take commerce and it tells us, if we get rates, how to pay it and how to save up and things like that. I don't think things like that would be taught at Lime School, not to a great extent anyway.

Pursuing the educational argument, a 14 year-old with muscular dystrophy commented

> I suppose if you've got a good brain and you really want to work at it, I think

this is the best school for it. You can work for 'O' levels and 'A' levels, which is what I want to do. At the other school you do learn a lot ... (but) they don't do public exams there.

This meant, according to another pupil, that

When you go for a job the person might say 'sorry, we can't have you because you haven't got any qualifications.' That's not the person's fault, it is because they were in a special school.

Besides qualifications, a majority of children stressed the greater normality of ordinary schooling, and the way it provides a better preparation for later life.

When you're at Lime School you're just part of everyone else. You don't care whether you're handicapped or what you can't do. Because nobody else cares. So if you come with normal kids, well you wouldn't get the understanding really. And I think that might be a bit awkward.

claimed one pupil, while another, talking about a friend who had remained at the special school, said

Well, when I saw him before, he said he didn't quite like it. They're all acting like babies. He wants to go to a proper school and do good work like other people, try to do what they can do, that kind of thing.

Another child made a similar point when she said that she thought ordinary education is best

Because it seems like a grown-up school. Sometimes people don't know that I'm handicapped.

Overwhelmingly then, children who had been selected for transfer from special to ordinary schooling were both personally pleased with the move and generally in favour of integration. Nevertheless, as pointed out before, they tended to be aware of the fact that some children—especially those with very severe physical disabilities, or those who would have difficulty in keeping up with lessons—might, in some ways, be better off in special provision. For this reason several respondents said they thought that individual children should have a choice about their schooling.

The consequences for able-bodied peers
Comments about the benefits of integrated education for the normalization of disabled pupils of course apply with almost equal force to the case of the able-bodied. We did not systematically ask all children what they thought the advantages and disadvantages would be for children already in ordinary schools if disabled pupils were introduced, but we did collect a number of comments on this question from ordinary primary school children and from both able-bodied and disabled comprehensive school pupils.

The junior school children, on the whole, made rather obscure comments about effects on able-bodied children, tending to say such things as

I'd be very nice to them, but some of them won't be.

or

When the handicapped children wanted to go somewhere, the ordinary children could help them.

In general these children did not seem to grasp other ways in which they might be affected although one boy did think that

> People might say that they've got crippled people in their school and it's a dumb school—that's what they might say.

and another felt that children would 'just laugh' if there were disabled pupils in his school.

Older children at the comprehensive schools had more to say on this question, although many did not seem to think that integration would really make any difference to anyone but the disabled. As one articulate boy put it:

> I don't think there are any advantages or disadvantages because you're going to meet people like that anyway sometime unless you happen to be very lucky or unlucky, depending on how you look at it. You might say you might as well meet them at school and get used to the fact there are people like that.

Nevertheless other pupils felt differently. One said

> Well, it might make a difference to some people because they might feel sort of differently if they have handicapped people in the school.

although he was not able to explain more specifically quite what he meant. Perhaps he was trying to make the point made by a peer:

> You know, when I get home I think about it. You know they can't walk.

Disabled children themselves sometimes also mentioned how integration might affect thé able-bodied. A 15 year-old with muscular dystrophy, for instance, emphasized how mixed schooling helps all pupils to realize the existence of physically disabled children:

> And when we go to the special schools they don't see a handicapped person, and so they think we're different. Of course we're not really.

Apart from effects on attitudes, integration of the physically disabled can have more practical consequences for pupils in general. Having to wait longer for individual attention, and jealousy at not being allowed to use the lift, were examples of ways in which able-bodied pupils felt they might have suffered because of integration. However, most crucial in this context, judging from comments, is that there are at least certain occasions on which the able-bodied and disabled pupils are treated differently.

Discipline, for instance, was apparently not uniformly applied to the two groups of pupils. At least two of the able-bodied children mentioned that the disabled pupils were more likely than the others to avoid detentions and reprimands. As one boy said about himself in relation to the boy with cerebral palsy in his class,

> I'm definitely more likely to get told off. Because if I get the bus and the bus is late that's just hard luck, you see. He usually gets away with it. He nearly always does if he's late because they take it that the bus was late. With me they always say I haven't got any excuse really. They say I should have got up and got a different bus.

Such practices of differential treatment seemed to be resented by both sides alike. This became clear when a 15 year-old with muscular dystrophy told us:

> I find at the moment that teachers seem to be afraid of telling us off. I'm ten minutes late for a lesson—alright, I might have gone to the toilet and it takes longer because Miss——has to take me. I should be asked 'Why?' I haven't got any excuse to be late. Even if they just asked me it would make other kids see I'm normal. You see, I know how they feel. I used to walk, and when I first went to Lime School I used to see kids coming in late for lessons and you used to say if he can be late, why can't I be late? It's like that. But, I mean, what do you expect them to say? ... I've been 20 minutes late for a lesson and they ain't said nothing. For being 20 minutes late they should have a go at me. They should even give me lines for it because I mean I haven't got any excuse being 20 minutes late. It's my own fault. Of course some of us take advantage of it. Why should they bother being on time when they're not going to get into trouble for it? But I don't look at it like that.

Summary

Most of the 88 children we spoke to seemed reasonably happy with their current schools, although just over a quarter did say they would like to go to a different school. The senior pupils at the special school were most likely to wish for transfer (four in ten indicated they would like a change, many saying they would prefer to attend an ordinary school) and the seniors at the comprehensives were least likely to want to move (none of the able-bodied, and only one of the disabled, pupils in this group wished to change schools).

Views on the relative advantages and disadvantages of special and ordinary education for disabled pupils were gained from all children including those who had personally experienced both types of schooling. The junior children and the senior pupils at the special school were most likely to favour segregation, and the pupils at the comprehensives—whether or not they had physical impairments themselves—most clearly saw the advantages of integration.

5 Friends and social activities

It is often said that disabled children have more difficulty than others in forming and maintaining friendships, and that their social life in general is far more restricted. In this chapter we examine these claims from the point-of-view of the children. We were particularly concerned to find out where pupils made friends, and to discover how far the social relationships of disabled children were disrupted by teasing. We also wished to find out the extent to which friendships at school were continued out of school hours. Finally, we were interested in how often different groups of children went out socially and in the activities in which they participated.

Friends at different schools
First of all we asked pupils whether they had friends at their own and at other schools. Their responses are shown in Table 15. As can be seen, the disabled pupils—and surprisingly perhaps, particularly those in the integration scheme—were considerably more likely than the non-disabled children to have friends only at their own school.

Characteristics of group	Friends at own school		Friends at own and other schools		Total
	No.	% of group	No.	% of group	
Able-bodied					
Juniors	—	—	16	100.0	16
Seniors	3	25.0	9	75.0	12*
Physically disabled					
Juniors in special education	17	58.6	12	41.4	29
Seniors in special education	8	47.1	9	52.9	17
Seniors in integrated education	10	76.9	3	23.1	13
Total	38	43.2	49	55.7	87

*One pupil claimed to have only a friend at another school.
Table 15: Friends from different schools

All the juniors in ordinary education said they had friends who went to other schools, and these friendships appeared to have arisen in a variety of ways. One girl told us of

> Lisa, she's a girl...me Mum works at this place in the afternoons and she comes there with her Mum as well. And we do different things. Sometimes we play badminton, sometimes we play 'he' or something.

while another reported that

> There's the little girl who's deaf. Her name is Debbie. I see them quite a lot—go over the park and play.

and a ten year-old boy said

> I've got some other friends, yeah. They go to a different school. They're my brother's friends.

If these children at the ordinary primary school are compared with the juniors in special education, a very different picture is found. Seventeen of the 29 disabled children in this age group had friends only at their own school. In other words, all the friends of these children were also physically disabled. One pupil, a ten year-old boy with spina bifida, confided that he had a girlfriend called

> Mandy. She's in my class. She's my girlfriend so she's rather special. She's the most special one of the lot. Loads of people want to get her, but at the moment I'm having the most luck. At least, I hope I'm having the best luck.

However the remaining twelve children in this group had 'normal friends', as a girl with cerebral palsy described them. One was an eight year-old boy with spina bifida, who mentioned

> Simon, my next-door neighbour and my friend where I used to live, he goes to an ordinary school...Sometimes they come round to my house and sometimes I go to their house.

At the secondary level, nine of the 13 able-bodied seniors had friends both at their own comprehensive school and at other schools, three said that they had friends only at the school they were currently attending, and one girl claimed only to have a friend at another school. The situation was rather different for the physically disabled seniors in integrated education, as only three out of 13 pupils reported friendships with pupils from schools other than their own. The remaining ten said they had friends at their own school only, although it was evident that some had contacts with other children even if these could not be classified as friendships. As one boy said in talking about pupils from his old school

> I only go down there (Lime School) once a week to go swimming, so I only see them once in a while. It's not so easy to keep friendships going like that.

Reference to Table 15 shows that the proportion of disabled seniors in special education with friends only at their own school was less than for the juniors at the same school, and that half these seniors had friends attending other schools—considerably more than among the group of integrated disabled seniors. However it is important to bear in mind that whereas there were approximately 1,200 pupils at each of the comprehensive schools involved in the integration scheme, junior and secondary level pupils at the special school together numbered only about 60. In other words, the potential choice of friends at the special school was very limited compared to the choice possible at the comprehensives.

All the disabled special school seniors nonetheless had at least one friend at their school. For a 14 year-old

> They are all very good friends to me. The best one is Paul...A couple of months ago I slid along the floor and broke me foot. Paul...saw me to the hospital and he stayed there with me for about three hours...He just wouldn't stop visiting me—he came nearly every day. That's what I like about him.

Likewise a girl with cerebral palsy said

> I've got quite a few girl friends. They help me out and I give them help if we need help or whatever.

Indeed, several of these pupils who had previously been to ordinary schools mentioned that they found it easier to make friends with disabled children. A 13 year-old with a blood disorder described the contrast for him between schools:

> At ordinary school when I'm going down the stairs, all the boys come and push me down. Here at school I could talk to friends and they don't make a fuss of it and we get on nicely.

These comments were echoed by a girl with epilepsy:

> This is the first school where I've ever settled down and get on with people so well...I had this girl—we used to be good friends when I went to the other school, but not really no more...I don't think she wants to talk to me no more because I've got the fits and go to a disabled school.

Reciprocated friendships

All the children were asked to name their 'special friends' at school. Most pupils could give the name of at least one child, and a few provided a long list of names. Some respondents, however, and in particular the older able-bodied and disabled adolescents at the comprehensive schools, were anxious to qualify their responses. Thus one told us

> The sixth form's quite small and you get to know everybody quite quickly.

while others said

> No one I could really, really trust.

and

> You can't really say in the fourth year you've got a best friend because the class is split up for every lesson. You're never—only one lesson you're in the classroom together.

Nevertheless only two able-bodied and three disabled (two at ordinary secondary schools and one at the special school) were unable to name any friends at school.

The information obtained in this way was used to examine friendship patterns in the schools. At the special school we talked to the majority of pupils and so we could consider the patterns in most detail and, in particular, we could see how far friendship choices were reciprocated. Using a 'sociometric' technique for examining the informal structure of groups first devised by Moreno (1934), we therefore compared the names of friends given by each pupil with the responses given by these 'friends' mentioned. This analysis was carried out for Red Class, in which children ranged in age between ten and 12 years, with an average age of just over 11 years. The findings are shown in Figure 2.

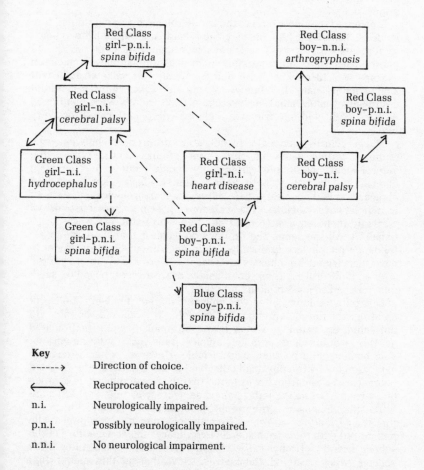

Key

------>   Direction of choice.

<------->   Reciprocated choice.

n.i.   Neurologically impaired.

p.n.i.   Possibly neurologically impaired.

n.n.i.   No neurological impairment.

Figure 2: Friendship choices made by Red Class (average age 11 years).

A number of physically disabled children have an impairment which involves some brain abnormality. At the special school in our study, 25 of the 46 children we spoke to were neurologically impaired, a further 15 were thought by the headteacher to be possibly impaired in this way, and only six children definitely had no neurological impairment. As a number of writers have indicated that children with brain disorders find it particularly difficult to make and maintain friendships, partly because they may exhibit associated characteristics such as hyperactivity, limited attentiveness, poor motor co-ordination, perceptual difficulties and mood changes, we were interested to compare the friendship patterns of these groups of pupils.

It emerged that, on average, the 24 neurologically impaired children made 2.52 friendship choices and had one friendship choice reciprocated for every 3.32 friends mentioned. By contrast, the 15 pupils who were only possibly neurologically impaired made an average of 2.13 choices, with one friendship reciprocated for every 2.66 friends named. Finally, among the six children without neurological impairment, an average of 2.33 friends were mentioned by each child and one friendship choice was reciprocated for every two made.

These figures conceal considerable differences between the children within each of the three groups. Thus, within the 'neurological impairment' group, one child made two friendship choices and had them both reciprocated while another made four choices and had none returned. Moreover, as neurological impairment is not always obvious, the category 'possibly impaired' almost certainly included a mixture of children who were and were not so impaired. All the same, the findings do suggest that there may be a tendency for physically disabled children without brain disorders to have their friendship choices reciprocated more readily than children with such disorders. These conclusions are, however, based on small numbers and so must remain tentative.

Less detailed information was collected on the friendship choices of children at the comprehensive schools. It was not possible to determine the extent to which friendship choices were reciprocated as this would have entailed much larger-scale interviewing of able-bodied children than was feasible. However, when friendship choices made by the physically disabled group and their non-disabled peers were considered, it was found that the former named an average of 2.1 friends while the latter named an average of 1.69. Perhaps more interesting, however, is the proportion of disabled students indicating that their friends were drawn from the group of disabled pupils who had moved with them from special to ordinary education: a third of the school friends of physically disabled children in the integration scheme were disabled themselves. Nevertheless this meant that two-thirds of their friends were non-disabled, and is a further indication that the majority of the disabled children placed at the comprehensive schools did mix socially and successfully with the able-bodied children at their school.

Making friends at integrated schools

It could be argued that any attempt to evaluate the 'success' of a scheme to integrate physically disabled children into mainstream education should take into account the children's ability to make friends under such conditions. In an earlier chapter we noted that about half the comprehensive school pupils mentioned the benefits of physically disabled and able-bodied children mixing socially at integrated schools. Here we turn to the related question of just how successful at making friends the disabled integrated pupils in fact were. This is a difficult issue to resolve, but a partial answer can be provided by considering how many of the pupils apparently made friends with their able-bodied peers.

In all it seemed that seven of the 13 pupils in question had 'integrated friendships' at their secondary school. A 14 year-old boy with muscular dystrophy in a wheelchair remarked

> I've a lot of friends really. I was really surprised when I came here. I thought I was going to be one person—nobody knew me and I didn't know anyone else. But I've got a lot of friends, not only in my own class—other classes, other years. I was surprised about that. How quickly you get to know people in a big school like this.

He continued

> My friends push me most of the time—come up with me (in the lift): I can't reach the button...What I mean by independent is just me and my friends, Not teachers.

Nevertheless several disabled children reported difficulties, at least at first, in making friends with other members of the school. The youngest girl in the integration scheme, with spina bifida, described her period of adjustment:

> I've got more friends here than I had at Lime School. I had friends but I'm better at mixing here...I tried to mix here and I mixed in with other friends because I didn't want to stay inside with the others all the time...Some of them are, a bit—you know—they stare at you and all that, but I just don't take no notice...Then after a while they make friends with you and then they're alright afterwards.

Other pupils felt that the difficulties they faced stemmed directly from having previously attended a special school. One commented

> I don't know how children in this school are because I've been to a handicapped school for a long time. I don't know how they react and all that. So we just have arguments.

A 15 year-old boy with muscular dystrophy also admitted that there were problems to be faced when he first joined the school:

> I didn't want to come at that time. Because it was new to me, and well, once I got here the first half of the year was the hardest time—trying to mix with the others. Because when you're at Lime you lose touch with people. When you come to a school like this you've got—I mean you get—an attitude where you think people should feel sorry for you and things like that. But now, after I've been here a few years, I'm just like one of the other pupils.

Some of these difficulties were noted by the non-disabled pupils. According to a 14 year-old

When they (the disabled children) get out of the special schools they have to stay within their group because they're too shy to go into other groups. They think that 'I can't do this, I can't do that' and they just go into a corner and stay there wrapped up in themselves...There's an advantage in one way in that if the normal children go and help, these children develop their social attitudes.

Of the six integrated pupils who appeared to be less successful than the other seven in forming friendships with able-bodied children, three seemed to have trouble making friends in general. We were told by a 15 year-old with spina bifida and hydrocephalus that

I don't make friends very easily. If I don't feel like talking to them and they start talking to me, I get aggressive. They keep on and on. I said I don't feel like talking. They hear what I said but they keep on and on and on. I just tell them where to go.

A slightly younger boy, also with spina bifida, confided

I can't get on with very much friends...They just sort of ignore me, you know. Sometimes they might come up and call me a few horrible things, but otherwise they just leave us alone. If they start an argument I finish it by running into their legs with the chair. You see, that finishes it.

The remaining three pupils had, however, formed friendships with other disabled members of the school. A 15 year-old boy in a wheelchair described how such friendships could develop:

At playtimes we play amongst ourselves because we play different from everybody else. Like they'll chase each other—we'll pretend to fight. We wouldn't hurt each other, we just muck about. And, well, we can't muck about like that with normal people, it's just what we're used to. There's about four of us who usually go round together. Timothy's not really handicapped, he's just got a bad heart really. I don't know why he came to our group, it just sort of happened. He said that he hasn't got many friends with the people in his class in the school. He's starting to make friends now, but slowly. But I did tell him that at any time he wanted to go off on his own to make other friends. I said 'Well you might as well go and do it.' I mean it's alright having a few friends, but you want as many friends as you can get really.

What emerged from our discussions was, as might be expected, that some integrated disabled pupils were better than others at forming friendships with able-bodied peers. Clearly a number of factors come into play here. A child's ability to form friendships may be affected by his personality, his educational performance and social skills *in addition* to the nature of, and his attitude towards, his physical disability. It was evident that the difficulties faced by some of the physically disabled children were *not* necessarily due solely to their handicap. Moreover it is important that only one of the 13 disabled pupils in the integration scheme stated a clear preference to be at another school.

Teasing
Friendship patterns can be markedly affected by teasing, and we now consider such behaviour in more detail. What we asked children on this issue varied slightly according to circumstances: able-bodied juniors were asked whether they thought disabled children would be

teased if they attended an ordinary school, while able-bodied seniors (those at the integrated schools) and the physically disabled subjects were asked if they had witnessed or experienced such unpleasant behaviour at school or out of school. As Table 16 shows, older pupils were more likely than younger pupils to say that teasing occurred. It is also worth noting that more disabled pupils reported problems of teasing when specifically asked about these than when they were given the opportunity to mention consequences of personal disability more spontaneously (see Table 9).

Characteristics of group	Teasing mentioned		Teasing not mentioned		Total
	No.	% of group	No.	% of group	No.
Able-bodied					
Juniors	4	25	12	75	16
Seniors	8	61.5	5	38.5	13
Physically disabled					
Juniors in special education	10	34.5	19	65.5	29
Seniors in special education	10	58.8	7	41.2	17
Seniors in integrated education	10	83.3	2	16.7	12*
Total	42	48.3	45	51.7	87

*One pupil did not answer this question.

Table 16: Teasing and the disabled child

Three-quarters of the non-disabled juniors, asked how they thought children at their school would react to physically disabled pupils, anticipated no particular problems. The remaining children, however, saw potential difficulties, and thought some disabled pupils might be teased.

The majority (19 out of 29) of the physically disabled juniors in special education, like the able-bodied, did not mention teasing as a problem. And for the rest, it seemed that teasing was more of a problem out of, than in, school. A ten year-old explained

> Outside friends are bullies. They come over and say all sorts of things that I don't like. So really I don't do a lot with them.

Other children, too, avoided contact with 'outside friends' because of teasing. Some, however, adopted other tactics:

Sometimes they tease me. They say 'come and play with me' and they never played with me. And I tried to tease them. I said 'come and play with me' and then I didn't play with them. So I teased them back.

A few children managed to cope with teasing through outside help. A nine year-old with spina bifida, for instance, received support from his brother

Some people say that I've got 'small legs', 'small feet', 'little legs'. Once when this boy said it to me, me brother beated him up and he was about fifteen. The brother beated him up for me.

Seven of the ten junior children who indicated that they had been teased were disabled by cerebral palsy. As there were 11 children with cerebral palsy of junior age at the special school, this means that almost two-thirds—a much higher proportion than for any other type of handicap—reported teasing. These children had neurological abnormalities as well as a physical handicap, and it is tentatively suggested that they may have been more likely than other groups to be subjected to teasing.

As has already been noted, a quite different impression of teasing emerges at secondary school level: a majority of each group of seniors—able-bodied and disabled in both integrated and special schooling—had witnessed or been the object of such unkind behaviour.

Eight of the 13 able-bodied seniors mentioned that the disabled pupils at their comprehensive school were teased. Several seniors emphasized that this was something that new disabled pupils might particularly expect, and a 13 year-old boy elaborated on the basis of his own experience:

I should think that in that first week or so there was a fair bit. Because when I first got my glasses they all went 'Ha, ha, four eyes' for about a week or so, and then they all shut up because they all forgot about it. And that's how I think it probably was with them.

An older girl confirmed this impression:

I suppose there is (teasing) sometimes, but I don't think they do a lot. I suppose some people do it, yeah, I think they do a little bit, but not as much as people would think they do.

Sometimes it appeared that teasing took the form of imitating the way a disabled child walked, or laughing when he or she fell over. In other cases it seemed to be a form of resentment. One pupil suggested that

Perhaps it's because they're in a wheelchair and they're lazy and that. They probably get off detentions and that because they're in a wheelchair.

Another pupil made the point that he felt the disabled children in the integration scheme needed to be resilient and determined:

If some one was very shy, and within the first week or so people teased them—they usually do—or maybe they laughed sometimes, and if they were very shy and sort of self-conscious type of person, then they might not fit in very well. And then you have to pretty well not have very many feelings because this is not a very considerate area—sort of rough and ready. People tend to be rather thick-skinned, you see. They don't mean to hurt people's feelings half the time, but half the time they do! You have to be able to fend for yourself. If someone was particularly sensitive and sort of self-conscious, I can't think they'd fit in very well.

The senior children in integrated education did indeed confirm that they experienced teasing. Over three-quarters of the disabled children at the comprehensives mentioned that they had been teased by fellow pupils or in the street, and in most cases this took the form of name-calling.

> It's always the same thing—'peg leg', 'Ironside'—you know it's always the same things and you get really irritated.

said a 17 year-old, while a younger pupil complained

> Some people call me 'shrimp' because I'm the smallest in the class. And they call me 'spastic legs', and I don't like it.

Several pupils said that they were referred to in a derogatory sense as 'spastic' when in fact their disability was spina bifida or polio. A 15 year-old girl explained

> Because children here don't know all the different types of handicap, they used to say 'Oh, you're spastic, right?' and they didn't know what it meant...That's about the only thing they know.

It seemed, from our conversations, that most integrated disabled pupils had been teased, at least during their first few weeks at the comprehensive school. However things usually got better in time. A 15 year-old told us he was not teased any more

> Because they've got used to me. But when I first came, of course they were bound to.

A pupil who had been at the comprehensive school for four years added

> When we used to come here, not so much myself, but some other people came here who were worse off than I am, you know, they used to really get it bad...But, I think now it's beginning to settle down.

Seven out of the 13 disabled pupils at comprehensive schools appeared to have made friends with able-bodied children. Of these seven, three made no mention of teasing, three emphasized that it was something experienced only when they first arrived at the secondary school, and one was currently still being teased. Of the six children who appeared to be less well integrated, four were still being teased when we spoke to them while two—both of whom had formed friendships with physically disabled peers—felt that teasing had been a problem only at first. We got the impression that it was the disabled pupils who were less successful in forming friendships with either able-bodied or disabled pupils who were the most likely to continue to be teased for a prolonged period following integration.

Nevertheless most integrated pupils did get teased at some time or another, and some described the ways that they coped with this unpleasant behaviour. Children said:

> I just call them names back.

or

> I just walked away. I don't look at them.

or

> It don't worry me.

Other pupils seemed more upset by teasing and less able to deal with it. In the words of a 13 year-old:

> I wear a sort of hearing aid in this ear. They come up to me...and they turn it up and shout in it, sort of laugh...I don't like wearing it because I don't like it when people turn it up...I get very annoyed. The children, they sort of make fun of you, make you feel upset about it...I get a bit upset, yes. Sometimes...I go up to them and say I'm going to beat you up, but I know I can't. I just try and act as tough as them.

An interesting question is whether more or less teasing takes place in integrated than in special education, and we were able to gain some insight on this from the children who had attended both kinds of school. The general consensus among such children was that there was substantially less teasing at the special school: eight children gave this impression, two mentioned teasing only at the comprehensive school, two did not mention teasing in either context, and in one case the question was not asked.

The feeling of a common identity at the special school seemed to inhibit teasing. Respondents explained that

> They're all handicapped there. I said you can't say much about yourself 'cos we're all handicapped.

and

> No, it didn't happen to me at all because most of us were alike anyway. What's there to say? But in this school they see you're different from them—like you could wear glasses—and they'd be calling you names.

All the same, there were at least 14 different types of physical disability among the children we talked to, and it simply was not true to say that 'most of us were alike anyway.' Nevertheless there did appear to be a common understanding of what it was like to be 'different' and a tacit agreement that teasing was not an acceptable form of behaviour at the special school.

This impression was generally supported by senior pupils at the special school. A 15 year-old with spina bifida told us that teasing was

> Not at this school because they're all like this. I mean you can't.

It appeared, in the majority of cases, that where teasing occurred—and it was reported far more often by seniors than by juniors in special education—it took place, unlike for the integrated pupils, out of school. In such instances the seniors tended to regard children who teased them as uninformed rather than deliberately unkind. A girl with epilepsy confided

> They used to, some of the kids...next door, say 'Oh, you go to a handicapped school', but they got over it. They don't bother me no more, because their parents speak to them about it.

A 14 year-old boy with muscular dystrophy pointed out that those who tease tend to be

Little kids—only the little ones, because they don't understand what's wrong with you...they laugh at you when you go past. I just go away from them. It is hard.

Methods of dealing with such hurtful behaviour were fairly limited. The feelings of a boy with spina bifida were that

If someone teases me a lot...it's no good taking notice and getting upset.

while the attitude of another was

But I can't do anything, can I?

A 15 year-old girl with cerebral palsy said

Quite a lot of kids laugh at you and say 'Oh, look at her'. But me—it doesn't bother me. I forget about it.

In conclusion it must be recognized that teasing of disabled children does occur both in and out of school, and that older pupils, and those in integrated schooling, are particularly likely to come across such behaviour. Nevertheless it does also seem that teasing decreases as able-bodied children get to know their disabled peers as classmates or neighbours, and it is encouraging to note that despite possible adverse social reaction, most disabled respondents welcomed contact with able-bodied children in both educational and social contexts.

Meeting friends out of school
Are friendships developed at school continued in out-of-school hours, and if so how? The main findings are presented in Table 17 (p.76) and show that the disabled pupils, and strikingly those attending the special school, were much less likely than the rest to see friends other than at school.

All the non-disabled junior pupils saw friends out of school, and in 14 out of 16 cases friends seen included children from other schools. For most children at this neighbourhood school, living nearby meant they tended to know other local children who also went to the same school. A nine year-old girl explained how easy it was to see her friends:

Sally...lives right opposite the school. I just come round the corner. Sometimes she comes round my house. Sometimes I see a boy named Richard in my class, and Tina and Wayne—I just see them in the street.

It was likely not only that these children would meet each other casually—'I just bump into them'—but also that they could visit each other's homes on their own without needing to be 'taken' by an adult. In this way friendships could be maintained and friends seen on the initiative of the children themselves. There were undoubtedly restrictions on where they could go and what they could do, but within these limits the able-bodied junior age children were relatively free to see their friends when they wished. This was clearly indicated by a nine year-old boy talking about his companions:

I go to their houses sometimes. Sometimes after school I go to Ray's house just to stick football stickers in a book. Or sometimes I go to William's house to play Family He—sometimes on Saturdays and Sundays when I haven't got anything to do, and sometimes he comes to my house.

The junior children in special education were in a very different situation. Nearly half appeared to see no friends at all outside school, whether these were from their own or other schools. Furthermore, only nine saw friends from the same school. The remaining six children saw friends from other schools only.

There are various reasons for the low level of social contacts shown by these children. In part, the wide catchment area of the school, spanning three London boroughs, was responsible. A ten year-old girl was in no doubt of the problems she faced when she said

This school is a long way—it should be a bit nearer to my home.

The point was elaborated by a nine year-old with spina bifida who told us

I'd like to see Val more often and all the rest of my friends...but we don't know where any of them lives.

Another junior, asked whether he saw school friends out of school hours replied

Yes, I saw one. I saw Peter when I went shopping. He didn't see me. He went the other way and I went straight—that's why I missed him.

For the majority of children at the special school it did seem that it was simply a matter of chance if they met a friend from school. As a result, school-based activities were particularly important to these children, as were after-school clubs, visits to places of interest and organized holidays. Some pupils explained that these trips can provide an opportunity to meet friends out of school, and an eight year-old boy with cerebral palsy said that he saw his best school friend only 'when we go on holiday with the school'.

Just over half of the 29 younger disabled children in special education saw friends at home either from their own or from another school. However whether or not these juniors were able to go out often depended on the help of parents, especially mothers. This is illustrated by the contrasting situations of two girls at the school. One told us that

Sally (another pupil at Lime School) does live quite near me and her Mum is a friend of my Mum's.

while the other complained

I haven't got much friends nearby—all my other friends live too far—my Mum's always busy.

Mobility presented a problem to most of these children, over half using walking aids such as calipers, sticks, a wheelchair, crutches or a rollator. As a ten year-old with spina bifida explained

I can't go out on my own because I can't tip my wheelchair very well. I have to have an adult with me. As I say, it's very difficult.

In consequence, children often found that friends visited them rather than vice versa. A girl who used a rollator commented

My friends come to my house because I can't go to their house—my Mum and Dad ain't got a car.

Are similar differences found among older pupils? So far as the able-bodied seniors at the comprehensive schools are concerned, it is clear from Table 17 that nearly all these children saw friends outside school and that more than two-thirds saw friends from both their own and other schools. It should be noted, however, that the comprehensive schools had much larger catchment areas than the neighbourhood junior school. This is likely to explain the comments of a 14 year-old girl who said she did not see her best friend out of school

Because she lives about half an hour's walk away from my house.

and of a slightly younger girl who explained that

After school...I only play with Tina, my friend, because all the other children live round the school. I don't live round the school.

However it was usual for the able-bodied children to have at least some school friends living within easy walking distance. As a 13 year-old boy told us

There's a friend opposite my house. Every day I come to school with him. I see him every day.

In only two instances did geography prevent children in this group from meeting fellow pupils, and in one of these cases friendships were formed with children living locally but attending other schools.

Although slightly more disabled than able-bodied seniors in ordinary education saw no friends outside school (three, as compared with one, out of 13), in general the friendship patterns of these two groups were quite similar—especially when contrasted with the circumstances of seniors in special education—and the majority saw friends out of school. Many disabled pupils clearly very much enjoyed the opportunities they had to mix with able-bodied young people and to take part in activities normal for their age group. A 15 year-old girl with cerebral palsy described her friendship with three able-bodied girls:

We meet each other and go out places. But my friend Sharon doesn't join in so much—she's not allowed to by her parents, but Sally and Carol, we go to discos and clubs, things like that...If there's any difficulty my Mum or Dad will always pick us up, because at the moment it's a bit difficult getting on to buses with my crutches and that. Apart from that it's fine.

Another girl with arthrogryphosis similarly noted

We just go round looking at places, to shops, we go to their house and listen to records, go down the market, you know, go all over the place really.

Of course some disabled children at the comprehensive schools continued to have difficulties in visiting their friends that were similar to those described by the juniors at the special school. A disabled girl indicated the difficulties she faced when she asked a fellow disabled pupil to visit her:

I started going up Sam's house last Sunday...I asked him (to come to my) house)—he said 'no' because he can't get up the steps in his wheelchair. He's on the ground floor.

However, with the assistance of friends and the willingness of parents

Characteristics of group	See no friends outside school		See 'own school' friends only outside school		See 'other school' friends only outside school		See 'own and other school' friends outside school		Total
	No.	% of group	No.	% of group	No.	% of group	No.	% of group	No.
Able-bodied									
Juniors	—	—	1	6.3	1	6.3	14	87.5	16
Seniors	1	7.7	2	15.4	1	7.7	9	69.2	13
Physically disabled									
Juniors in special education	14	48.3	4	13.8	6	20.7	5	17.2	29
Seniors in special education	10	58.8	1	5.9	4	23.5	2	11.8	17
Seniors in integrated education	3	23.1	6	46.2	—	—	4	30.8	13
Total	28	31.8	14	15.9	12	13.6	34	38.6	88

Table 17: Contacts with friends outside school

to allow their children out with friends, unaccompanied by an adult, a number of these problems can be overcome. A 14 year-old boy in a wheelchair described how

> If friends come down to my house and then we decide to go to their house or to go out, then it's more difficult because I can't push myself. I've got to be pushed.

Friendships maintained out of school were sometimes between disabled and non-disabled pupils, and in these instances able-bodied children often visited their disabled friends. One non-disabled girl talked of such a friendship:

> Usually I go and see Tania, and if she's not there I go to my other friends.

When asked if Tania ever visited her, she replied

> No, because we've got a lot of stairs and she can't get up them.

Ability to meet friends socially was not, however, solely dependent upon personal mobility. None of the three disabled seniors in integrated eduction who saw no friends out of school used a wheelchair and, furthermore, all four pupils in wheelchairs at the comprehensive schools managed to see friends. It seemed that other factors were more important.

Finally, how far were the seniors remaining in special education able to meet friends outside school? Somewhat over half of these pupils said that they did not see any friends out of school except at after-school clubs organized in association with the special school, and of the remainder only three saw schoolfriends during evenings, weekends or holidays. On the basis of these observations it might seem that it becomes harder, not easier, for pupils at the special school to have contacts with friends as they reach adolescence.

For many of these seniors, difficulties in getting out were very similar to those described by younger pupils. Among the comments noting familiar problems were:

> I don't visit the friends that are in my school... because I don't live near them.

> When I had my party most of my friends are in wheelchairs and they can't fit through the door. My teacher might plan a party here.

and

> Christopher, he's got the same as me... He comes round my house. I go down his house quite a lot by my Mum's car.

Most of these pupils would have liked to see their friends more often than they were able to. A 15 year-old girl summarised what she thought she was missing:

> At school you can't talk like you could if you were at home. You can't have a real laugh. You can about some things, but it's mainly working here. But at home you can have a laugh and talk about what you want.

These seniors seemed more prone than other groups to feelings of depression as a result of their social isolation. A 15 year-old boy with spina bifida compared himself with able-bodied young people:

They go everywhere I can't—then I get miserable and I have to stay in.

These feelings were sometimes enhanced among children disabled as the result of an accident or the onset of an illness who could compare their own life 'before' and 'after'. A 15 year-old boy injured in a road traffic accident said poignantly but simply

I can't walk—my friends don't want to come.

The reasons behind the considerable difference in the social life of disabled children at the comprehensive and at the special schools are complex. In special, as in ordinary, education, use of aids did not appear to be a prime factor: four of the seniors at the special school used wheelchairs, but only two of these were among the ten pupils who did not see friends out of school, and six of these latter ten children did not use aids at all. It is possible that parental attitudes towards their teenage children may differ according to whether they attend 'sheltered' or 'open' schooling, just as the disabled child's tendency to rebel and assert his or her independence may be greater at a comprehensive school, encouraged by able-bodied peers. However this is simply speculation. All we can say with certainty is that the disabled seniors in comprehensive schools did often develop friendships which were sustained out of school hours, and that in this way they could be contrasted with the special school seniors. These differences are unlikely to be simply due to school placement. However integrated education did result in opportunities and changes in attitude which, for some children at least, contributed to a more varied and full social life.

Social activities

We asked pupils about their social activities out of school, and the frequency with which children said they went to clubs, were involved in sport, or attended church or religious meetings is shown in Table 18.

Senior pupils much more often than juniors, and disabled seniors more frequently than able-bodied seniors, belonged to clubs. Indeed only just over one in three of the able-bodied juniors were currently attending clubs. Of this minority, a nine year-old told us

I can go to an after-school club. I used to go a lot, but I don't go now because I think it's boring because it don't get opened on Saturdays. And I made an electric lamp. The only thing I like there is woodwork, that's all. The other big boys, they start fights sometimes.

and another pupil reported that

At the park there's a little club thing where we can do needlework, paint, do what we want... after school, in the holidays, anytime.

Other clubs mentioned included Brownies and Boys Brigade as well as various sports clubs for judo, weight-lifting, gym, snooker and table tennis. Several children mentioned that they had gone to clubs of this kind in the past, but that they were no longer doing so, usually because 'I don't feel like it'.

About the same proportion of juniors at the special school belonged to clubs, although they attended fewer different kinds. A Cub and

Characteristics of group	Clubs Mentioned		Not mentioned		Sports Mentioned		Not mentioned		Church Mentioned		Not mentioned		Total
	No.	% of group	No.	% of group	No.	% of group	No.	% of group	No.	% of group	No.	% of group	No.
Able-bodied													
Juniors	6	37.5	10	62.5	11	68.8	5	31.3	4	25.0	12	75.0	16
Seniors	7	53.8	6	46.2	11	84.6	2	15.4	4	30.8	9	69.2	13
Physically disabled													
Juniors in Special Education	10	34.5	19	65.5	11	37.9	18	62.1	12	41.4	17	58.2	29
Seniors in Special Education	12	70.6	5	29.4	7	41.2	10	58.8	6	35.3	11	64.7	17
Seniors in Integrated Education	10	76.9	3	23.1	8	62.5	5	38.5	8	61.5	5	38.5	13
Total	45	51.1	43	48.9	48	54.5	40	45.5	34	38.6	54	61.4	88

Table 18: Social activities

Brownie pack were based at the special school and several pupils returned to school in evenings or on Saturdays for these meetings. Some children managed to join integrated packs, and they were very pleased to be able to do so. Inevitably, however, they faced minor difficulties. A ten year-old girl with spina bifida in a wheelchair explained

> I'm a Brownie at the moment...There's only one handicapped—me. The Brownies like pushing me, but I don't like them doing it. They go too fast.

and a nine year-old who also had spina bifida, and who used calipers and crutches, said

> Sometimes I feel so left out. Especially when I go to Cubs every Monday...Some of the games I just can't join in, and in these situations I just feel *so* left out.

Apart from Cubs and Brownies, the only club mentioned by these junior pupils was one open to both physically disabled and able-bodied children. A ten year-old with cerebral palsy was particularly enthusiastic about this:

> Saturday club. (It's a) mixture really, handicapped and normal ones... We get out camping a lot and we get out more than if I went to a normal club. You get out a lot and you're never bored.

Just over half the non-disabled comprehensive pupils attended clubs—such as Scouts, a youth club, football training, shorthand and typing, dancing and gymnastics clubs—and more still had previously belonged to groups including Girls Brigade and a swimming club. Somewhat more disabled senior pupils, at both ordinary and special schools, were members of clubs.

Most of the older disabled pupils who attended clubs went to the local Physically Handicapped and Able-Bodied (PHAB) club—for which transport was provided—once a week after school. This club enabled the able-bodied to meet the disabled pupils from their own and other schools in a relaxed informal setting, and it also allowed the integrated pupils to meet their former friends from the special school. Generally this club seemed liked by the pupils. A 14 year-old with arthrogryphosis told us

> There's a senior club. Me and my friends go. It's PHAB...it's alright, it's good...We listen to records, muck about...because, you know, it's mixed in a way. It's more able-bodied there than handicapped. But I like it. My friends go as well. We enjoy ourselves.

Four disabled pupils at the comprehensive schools chose not to attend the PHAB club, and at least two indicated that they did not want to attend a club specifically for the 'physically handicapped'. However the majority view was expressed by a 15 year-old with muscular dystrophy:

> Yes, there's a club (PHAB) every Thursday. I meet old friends from Lime while I'm there and it's a bit of a laugh when you're there.

If school-based clubs (such as for electronics) are excluded, the only other clubs which the physically disabled pupils in integrated schools attended as members were Scouts and Guides. A 14 year-old boy with spina bifida who used a wheelchair told us

> I go to Scouts every Friday night—I'm the only handicapped person there. They just pull me in and I have to get going. Because anyway they know that my brother is there, so if any funny business goes on...But you know they're all my friends...I've been going since I was ten.

However, problems arose if he wanted to go on outings with the Scouts:

> If they take the Scout wagon with them, yes, but if they go on buses and coaches and what have you, I can't go then. Because then they have to get the chair out of the coach and what have you. And that's too much. I've been on day trips with them and I've done a camp cook badge, but I only went during the day.

This boy also attended another club, but in a different capacity:

> My mum used to do one on Saturdays and I used to go down there and give a hand. Try to teach them a few things. And Mum doesn't go any more, but I still go down there and teach them...Well they're severely mentally retarded so I get a load of jigsaws, very simple ones, and help them with those. They manage to play basketball quite a bit, which I've taught them. And my friend, he's quite often there, he does woodwork with them...I'm more or less a helper on Saturday.

By contrast, none of the seniors in special education attended any club or social meeting other than PHAB. Both by comparison with their disabled peers at the comprehensive schools, and particularly as compared with the able-bodied seniors, these pupils had restricted opportunities to meet other adolescents socially at the clubs and groups aimed at young people of their age.

We judged that a child had an interest in sporting activities if playing sports, such as football or rounders, out of school hours, or attending matches or other events as a spectator, were mentioned. Table 18 shows that able-bodied pupils mentioned interests of this kind more frequently than the disabled, although participation in sporting activities was more common among the integrated seniors than among the other groups of disabled pupils.

Whereas 11 of the 16 able-bodied juniors played or watched sports in their spare time—usually football—only 11 of the 29 disabled juniors enjoyed these activities as either a spectator or a participant. Among this latter minority there were, nonetheless, some enthusiasts. A nine year-old boy with spina bifida who used calipers and a rollator told how

> I can still play football...I can be the goalkeeper and be defenser. Today I played football and I scored a goal.

This boy also enjoyed using a skateboard:

> I can easily do it. Some people say I can't but I can. Just put it in front of my wheel and go along and it goes with the wheels.

At the comprehensive schools, nearly all the able-bodied seniors were interested in a wide variety of sports including football, cross-country running, ice-skating, badminton and swimming. To be not interested in sports was very much the exception, as one 13 year-old boy indicated:

No, I'm not interested in sports—unlike everyone else around here. They're absolutely crazy about Tottenham or Arsenal or whatnot.

Just under two in three of the physically disabled seniors at these schools enjoyed sporting activities. Several of the most frequently mentioned sports had a therapeutic value such as strengthening muscles, as well as providing pure fun. A 15 year-old girl with cerebral palsy told us

> I enjoy swimming quite a bit and, hopefully, when it gets warmer, once my legs get a bit stronger, I will start horse riding again. I used to horse ride quite a few years ago, and we had a few problems and then I had to stop for a little while. Now I'm hoping to start again. I'm looking forward to that. It should be nice.

Some seniors whose disabilities made it difficult for them to participate in sports nonetheless enjoyed going to football matches as spectators. A 14 year-old boy with muscular dystrophy who was wheelchair-bound said he had

> ...been to a few matches. I've been to one with my Dad and to about three or four with my friends. My friends are very good like that—they take me out places. I've been to the football match with them. And they're very good at the Spurs. They let me in through the back entrance...and give me a good seat.

At the special school, seven out of 17 pupils expressed an interest in sporting activities. Here, in particular, were a number of children who had to face reductions in their physical ability either following a road traffic accident or as a result of a deterioration in their condition. For some of these children it seemed that perhaps sports were a painful reminder of their previous state. A 14 year-old boy with muscular dystrophy exclaimed

> I don't like sport. I think it's a load of rubbish.

Moreover the difficulties faced in pursuing her favourite sport were described by a 13 year-old with spina bifida and hydrocephalus:

> I used to go riding, but since I had my back operation I wasn't able to go because it was hurting...My back was curving so I had to go and have it straightened and hopefully when I get my corset off I can go back to riding.

There was a particularly marked contrast between the able-bodied seniors and those at the special school in the popularity of sporting activities. The latter group, for reasons including personal preference, physical condition and problems of mobility and access, found it difficult to develop an interest in sports as either a participant or a spectator.

We also briefly examined how often pupils attended a church service or other religious meeting. Among the able-bodied, only four juniors and four seniors appeared to go to church at all regularly (at least attending the major festivals of the year). And among the physically disabled, less than half of the juniors attended a church or other religious service occasionally or more frequently. Often these visits seemed to reflect attendance at Cubs or Brownies where 'Church Parade' was organized. The disabled seniors at the special school went to services scarcely more often than the able-bodied group. However nearly two-thirds of the disabled seniors at the comprehensive schools did visit a church, mosque or other religious service. A 14 year-old Greek Orthodox girl confirmed that she and her family attended church:

> Oh yes, every Sunday if we can. And we go at Easter. We go one whole week, every night, and sometimes I go with my brother-in-law and stay in at night. And, you know, Easter, Christmas and special occasions we go.

It is difficult to say why the disabled seniors in integrated education were more likely than members of any other group of disabled or able-bodied pupils to attend church or other religious meetings. Given the relatively small number of pupils interviewed, we cannot judge whether some special characteristics of the integrated group were responsible or if, as seems more likely, the association was coincidental.

Summary

All the able-bodied juniors and the majority of the able-bodied seniors had friends at their own school and at other schools. Disabled seniors at the comprehensive schools tended to form friendships mainly with fellow pupils, and over half had close relationships with able-bodied peers. A minority of these seniors, however, experienced some difficulties in making friends, although usually this seemed due to a lack of social skills rather than because of their disability as such. Special school pupils were more likely than the integrated disabled seniors, but less likely than the able-bodied, to report friends at both their own and other schools.

One third of the able-bodied juniors, as compared with almost two-thirds of the able-bodied seniors, thought that disabled children were likely to be teased. Only just over a half of the disabled themselves said they had experienced such unkind behaviour, although these pupils were more likely to be older, and to attend an ordinary school. Whereas juniors in special education who mentioned being teased usually referred to instances out of school, many of the integrated disabled pupils told of teasing when they first joined the comprehensive school. However only a small minority of this latter group continued to be teased after the first few weeks at the school, and these pupils tended to be those who formed friendships less easily.

Contact with friends outside school varied considerably. All the able-bodied juniors and seniors saw friends out of school, as did almost all the integrated seniors. By contrast, nearly half the disabled juniors saw no friends out of school, and more than half the special school seniors were in the same position. Those who were able to meet friends relied heavily on help from adults, particularly mothers. It became harder, not easier, to develop and maintain social contacts as the disabled adolescents at the special school grew older.

There was, in general, more variety shown by the able-bodied than the disabled pupils in social leisure activities. Most disabled seniors attended a PHAB club, but few went to any other form of club or meeting. The able-bodied became increasingly interested in sport and more than half the integrated group had a similar interest. However only about four in ten seniors at the special school followed any sport.

6 Family and home life

Many disabled children find it difficult to go out in evenings and at weekends and few have many friends out of school. It is therefore of particular interest to find out more about their families and to ask whether they tend to go on outings with their parents and brothers and sisters and how they typically spend their leisure time at home.

The pupils' families

Before discussing family life in any detail, we first looked briefly at the composition of the children's families.

Table 19 indicates whether children came from one- or two-parent (not necessarily two natural parents) families, and it can be seen that the vast majority of both the able-bodied and the disabled pupils lived in two-parent units. As approximately 89 per cent of all families with dependent children in Great Britain in 1979 were two-parent units, while about 11 per cent were one-parent units (Central Statistical Office, 1981), it would seem that the proportion of single-parent families was around, or even below, the average in all groups except for the seniors in integrated education. Seven of these 13 pupils lived with two parents although the remainder did not. Five lived with one parent and one with neither.

Several writers have suggested that some types of handicap impose greater strains than others on family relationships and hence may be associated with higher rates of marital breakdown. The evidence from this study does not add support to this claim. Although the two children in the sample living with neither parent were both disabled, there was no suggestion *in general* that families containing disabled children were more likely to be split by separation or divorce than others. Moreover, so far as the disabled integrated pupils were concerned, we were not able to detect any marked similarities between the five families broken by separation or divorce (in the sixth case a parent had died) or to say to what extent, if at all, the child's disability contributed to the break.

Next, we examined the position of the children in their families— whether they were the first-born, youngest or oldest child, or if they were in the 'middle' of families. Certain differences were found between the disabled and non-disabled juniors (see Table 20) in that more than three times the proportion of the first group were eldest children and twice the proportion were only children. Amongst the seniors, both the able-bodied and the disabled pupils in integrated education were predominantly the middle or youngest members of

Characteristics of group	Two parents		One parent		Other		Total
	No.	% of group	No.	% of group	No.	% of group	No.
Able-bodied							
Juniors	14	87.5	2	12.5	—	—	16
Seniors	12	92.3	1	7.7	—	—	13
Physically disabled							
Juniors in special education	25	86.2	3	10.3	1	3.4	29
Seniors in special education	16	94.1	1	5.8	—	—	17
Seniors in integrated education	7	53.8	5	38.5	1	7.7	13
Total	74	84.1	12	13.6	2	2.3	88

Table 19: One- and two-parent families

their families. However the seniors in special education showed a different pattern and appeared to resemble the juniors at their own school as over a third were eldest born. There seemed, moreover, to be some association between birth order and disability. Less than half of all pupils in special education, but two-thirds of the first-borns in this group, had cerebral palsy. In addition, and by contrast, less than one in six children with spina bifida were the eldest in their families.

There is some evidence from other sources that a mother may be influenced against further pregnancies if she gives birth to a disabled child. It was not possible to investigate this possibility in the present study in any systematic manner. However it should be noted that six of the eight 'only' children we talked to were disabled, and perhaps in some of these instances a decision was made to have no further children. More generally, however, examination of this issue is complicated by the fact that at least 12 (one in five) of the disabled children had acquired rather than congenital disabilities; in these cases the onset of disability may have post-dated, rather than influenced, decisions about individual family size.

Effects of disability on the rest of the family.

We asked disabled children if they ever talked to their parents or brothers and sisters about their disability (see pages 30-32), but we did not question them directly on the effects that their disability had had on their families. Nevertheless several pupils did spontaneously mention that other members of their families had at various times been worried or upset by their condition.

Several pupils at the special school—six juniors and two seniors—commented on family worries. One nine year-old girl who was severely disabled following a road traffic accident told us that

> When I first had the accident, all my family cried.

while an 11 year-old with cerebral palsy said:

> It worries my Mum and Dad. My Dad's hair is going grey...He wants me to walk so we can go out....Now we can't go out a lot.

Several other children also indicated that their parents worried about their inability to walk and a ten year-old with spina bifida claimed

> My Mum does (worry) though. About me. She sometimes worries about me—getting me upstairs. I can just about manage it...My Mum or Dad always has to be with me...I don't actually walk upstairs because I've got a lift.

Amongst the older pupils, a 14 year-old girl with cerebral palsy and hydrocephalus commented on her disability:

> It worries my Mum. She wishes I could do all the housework for her. She could go out to work and she'd only have to come back in the evening. And she was saying to me 'Why didn't it turn out like that?'

Only two of the disabled adolescents at the comprehensive schools volunteered that their families were worried or upset—although that does not necessarily mean that there were no anxieties felt by others. In the words of one of these pupils, a 13 year-old with polio:

Characteristics of group	Oldest		Middle		Youngest		Only		Total
	No.	% of group	No.	% of group	No.	% of group	No.	% of group	No.
Able-bodied									
Juniors	1	6.3	4	25.0	10	62.5	1	6.3	16
Seniors	2	15.4	6	46.2	4	30.8	1	7.7	13
Physically disabled									
Juniors in special education	6	20.7	5	17.2	14	48.3	4	13.8	29
Seniors in special education	6	35.5	2	11.8	7	41.2	2	11.8	17
Seniors in integrated education	2	15.4	5	38.5	6	46.2	–	–	13
Total	17	19.3	22	25.0	41	46.6	8	9.1	88

Table 20: Position of child in family

I don't talk to my Mum about it (my disability) 'cos it gets her upset too. You know, ... she'll think it's her fault.

Sometimes it was clear that subjects wished to protect their families as far as possible. This seemed to be true of an eight year-old pupil who did not really want to have another operation (his eighth?) which might enable him to go to an ordinary school, but who apparently resigned himself to it with the consideration

What about my Mum? If I stay here (at special school) she's going to start crying—if the operation doesn't work.

Outings with parents
We have already discussed the frequency with which disabled and able-bodied children see friends out of school hours, and in this section we also consider social activities with families. In Table 21 we show the number of children who reported outings with friends* and with parents. Overall children were slightly more likely to go out with families than with friends, and this tendency was particularly marked for children in special education.

Almost all the able-bodied juniors we spoke to mentioned going out with friends. Nearly as many were also taken out by their parents. A ten year-old girl gave a clear picture of what happened in her family:

We go to places like Madame Tussauds or we go up London and look at different things. Or we go to see shows like the Harlem Globetrotters ... Not regular, but we do go out often. Like if my Dad says 'Right, we're going out', we just get everything ready and go. Or he'll surprise you. One Saturday when my Mum goes shopping very early she'll come back and we'll all go out.

Most of the juniors in special education also went out with their parents, although they were less likely to do so than the able-bodied. What is particularly striking within this group, however, is the contrast between going out with friends and parents. The disabled juniors were substantially less likely to go out with friends (less than half did so) than their able-bodied peers. As a result, many really seemed to look forward to going out with parents. A seven year-old girl with cerebral palsy told us

I go out with my Mummy, my Daddy and my brother, altogether and with me in the pram (major buggy?) because I can't keep my balance properly. We've got a dog too. We take it for a walk in the park ... the swings, the slide ...

Visits to the park or the cinema may not be arranged easily for some of the disabled, but it was evident that a number of parents went to considerable lengths to enable their child to participate as much as possible in activities usual for his or her age. A nine year-old boy with cerebral palsy was a film fan and described how

I saw *Grease* and *Jaws* with my Mum and my sister and me ... I leave the chair downstairs and my Mum carries me.

*Outings with friends are not synonymous with 'contact with friends' as shown in Table 17. 'Going out with friends' in Table 21 implies that a child goes outside his or her home together with friends.

Characteristics of group	Going out with friends at home				Going out with parents				Going out with brothers and sisters				Going out with brothers and sisters and their friends				Total
	Mentioned		Not Mentioned		Mentioned		Not Mentioned		Mentioned		Not Mentioned		Mentioned		Not Mentioned		
	No.	% of group	No.	% of group	No.	% of group	No.	% of group	No.	% of group	No.	% of group	No.	% of group	No.	% of group	No.
Able-bodied																	
Juniors	15	93.8	1	6.3	14	87.5	2	12.5	12	75.0	4	25.0	3	18.8	13	81.3	16
Seniors	11	84.6	2	15.4	10	76.9	3	23.1	8	61.5	5	38.5	3	23.1	10	76.9	13
Physically disabled																	
Juniors in special education	14	48.3	15	51.7	21	72.4	8	27.6	14	48.3	15	51.7	1	3.4	28	96.6	29
Seniors in special education	7	41.2	10	58.8	14	82.4	3	17.6	6	35.3	11	64.7	1	5.9	16	94.1	17
Seniors in integrated education	10	76.9	3	23.1	10	76.9	3	23.1	8	61.5	5	38.5	3	23.1	10	76.9	13
Total	57	64.8	31	35.2	69	78.4	19	21.6	48	54.5	40	45.5	11	12.5	77	87.5	88

Table 21: Going out at home with friends and family

Despite these efforts on the part of some families, over a quarter of the disabled juniors said they did not ever go on outings with their parents. The impact of such a restricted social life is considerable, especially as over half the disabled juniors did not go out with friends either.

Outings were much more common for the able-bodied seniors. Within this group of 13 pupils, 11 went out with friends and ten went out with parents. This pattern was almost exactly repeated by the physically disabled seniors at the comprehensive schools: ten out of 13 went out with friends and the same number said they went out with parents. Nevertheless disabled adolescents are often restricted, and a 15 year-old girl with spina bifida and hydrocephalus sounded a little disappointed when she said

> She (my mother) goes shopping with my sister. She does a lot of shopping for a month or something and there's a lot of heavy stuff to carry and she says I can't carry it. So I might as well stay at home. I'll do the tidying up and my sister will do the shopping.

The circumstances of the disabled seniors at the special school were quite different yet again. There was no evidence that these pupils found it easier to go out on their own with friends as they became older. Indeed, proportionately fewer seniors than juniors at the special school went out with friends, and more went out with their parents. Admittedly the different disabilities of the juniors and the seniors at the school (see Table 1), together with the deterioration in the physical condition of some children, may partly account for a reduction in the social activities of the seniors. Nevertheless the causes of limited outings are sometimes much more complex and can involve social as well as practical considerations. Whatever the reason, it was hard not to conclude that the seniors in special education were becoming more reliant on their parents for social outings at precisely the time when the able-bodied adolescents were beginnings to break their ties with home by spending more time with friends and establishing an independent life.

Brothers and sisters and their friends
Outings with brothers and sisters (and their friends) were less frequent than outings with either personal friends or parents. As Table 21 shows, going out with siblings was least likely of all for pupils in special education.

Three-quarters of the non-disabled pupils in ordinary education went out with their brothers and sisters although less than one in five went out with siblings plus friends. One nine year-old seemed rather lucky in these respects:

> Sometimes my brother takes me around on his motorbike. And my other one used to, but his bike's broken, so he takes me in his car...I go for a ride and my brother takes me and my mate up to his girlfriend's house and we play.

Not all children could, however, rely on older brothers and sisters who often had different interests. This was recognized by a ten year-old girl who told us:

> My brother's fifteen, and he likes going out on his own.

All the same, and despite their differences, most of the children appeared to get on reasonably well with their brothers and sisters, and arguments seemed to focus on which television programme to watch, name-calling and general bickering. A ten year-old girl fairly typically summed up her feelings towards her 11 year-old sister:

> Sometimes she's a nuisance, sometimes she's a nincompoop, sometimes she's alright.

Juniors in special education were not as likely as these able-bodied children to be included in the activities of their brothers and sisters. Less than half said they went out with siblings and there was only a single child who also met and went out with their friends. Part of this difference can nonetheless be attributed to the fact that four disabled juniors were 'only' children.

Although many of these pupils seemed to get on well with siblings, such as a nine year-old girl with spina bifida who walked with calipers and a rollator, and who said

> He (my brother) usually takes me out...I need someone to watch me, but I don't need anyone to help me 'cos I can get up and down the kerb by myself.

a few did mention irritations. It is not always easy to accept help, however well intentioned, and this probably affected the reaction of a nine year-old in a wheelchair. She said of her six year-old sister:

> She understands I can't walk, so sometimes she pushes me. It gets on my nerves...I like Mum pushing me, though.

Comparable feelings seemed to apply in the case of a ten year-old boy with cerebral palsy whose brother and sister were 14 and five years old respectively, and who reported that

> My brother and sister can write better than me and things like that. And they can do things better than I can. That's what I don't really like.

Of the older children, almost two-thirds of the non-disabled seniors went out with brothers and sisters and just under a quarter also went out with their friends. In the case of a 12 year-old

> Sometimes my sister takes me and me brother to the pictures or we go down the shops together. My sister goes out herself with her friends—discos and things.

Often it seemed that siblings had become less willing, as they grew older, to be joined in activities by a younger brother or sister. A 14 year-old girl no longer went out with her brother:

> No, because he always wants to go out with his friends and he never wants to take me. I used to, when he was about sixteen he used to take me swimming. But now he don't want to take me anywhere.

Exactly the same number of disabled as able-bodied seniors at the comprehensive schools (eight out of 13 in each case) went out with brothers and sisters. Indeed in many ways some of these disabled pupils seemed little different from their non-disabled peers. One 13 year-old girl with polio told us:

> They take me to the pictures, go to the funfair, they really treat me. They're the kind of sisters who don't treat me as if I'm handicapped. They act as if

I'm the same as them. Like my Mum now, she even hits me, you know. Some people think that as I'm like this, my Mum wouldn't hit me. I like her doing that just to say that I could be normal too.

In some cases it seemed that siblings were especially kind, and one or two disabled seniors received particularly generous presents from older brothers and sisters. An 11 year-old girl with spina bifida related how

My other brother, he really looks after me, he gives me everything. He gave me ear-rings, and he gave me money ... soap. I go to his house nearly every Sunday.

Some of these pupils also referred to being taken to the cinema and swimming by their brothers and sisters.

In three out of 13 cases—again the same number as in the able-bodied group—these disabled seniors said they were taken along when brothers and sisters went out with their friends. In the case of a 14 year-old boy with spina bifida:

We go to my brother's friend's house and my brother, his friends and me go down to the pictures or something ... Me and my brother's friends mix together although they're able-bodied. My brother has told them about me and they understand quite well. So I go out with them.

There may be all sorts of reasons why *any* brothers and sisters (disabled or not) do not spend their leisure time outside the home together, and five in each group at the comprehensive schools indicated that this was the case. However in one or two instances the disabled pupil felt this was directly related to his or her disability. A 13 year-old with cerebral palsy said

They never agreed to take me. They think I was slower. When I'm walking I'm sort of too slow, get out of breath easily. They don't bother.

Generally speaking, both the integrated disabled and the able-bodied seniors had their share of disagreements with siblings, although disputes were usually fairly trivial. As a 15 year-old non-disabled girl pointed out

You know all sisters have a row about something, don't they?

and this claim was supported by a girl of the same age at the same school who had cerebral palsy and who exclaimed

Arguments [laughs loudly]? *Definitely!* 'Can I borrow your clothes tonight?' 'No, you can't'. You know, very brother-and-sister like.

Only occasionally did it appear that the cause of a row was directly related to disability. This was, however, so for one girl who explained:

Sometimes it's all sorts of different things. Maybe sometimes I can't do the housework. Maybe they think—because I've got pains, you see—and maybe they think why does she not have to do it. Because they don't seem to understand that if I could do it, I would.

At other times the effects of disability may be indirect, and the frustration felt by a disabled young person may rebound on a brother or sister. A 15 year-old with spina bifida and hydrocephalus admitted

I kick my sister—she's got a lot of bruises on her legs ... I don't mean to, but she just annoys me so I kick her. Then I realise what I've done and I tell her I'm sorry.

Apart from a few exceptions, we did not get the impression that disabled children got on less well with their brothers and sisters than did other children.

Finally, how often did the physically disabled seniors in special education share activities with their brothers and sisters? Only just over a third said they went out with them as compared with nearly two-thirds of able-bodied and disabled seniors at the secondary schools. Even compared with the juniors at the same school, the disabled seniors fared particularly badly in this respect. Given this situation, it is perhaps not surprising that only one senior accompanied the friends of her sister on outings.

Among the luckier of these pupils, a 15 year-old boy with spina bifida, who used a wheelchair, told how his ten year-old brother would sometimes help him to get out:

My brother does—he can push me around ... He takes me around or pushes me around.... We usually go round the block. My mother won't let us go very far ... I ask him sort of every week. I ask him and he says 'No, not this time—next time' and sometimes I don't like it when he says that because I can't go out on my own ... I do ask him because there's nothing else I can do if I just stay at home ... I just sit at home, watch the television and be bored.

The need to be accompanied by someone on outings, either because pupils could not manage on their own or for the sake of safety, was not always readily accepted by brothers and sisters. Thus a 13 year-old with a blood disorder said of his brothers:

If I go out to play with them, they say they're going to the shops and I never see them again. So I have to go back in.

Indeed many pupils were dependent on their siblings for going out at all. The case of a 14 year-old with epilepsy is not atypical:

If my sister's going down to her friends, maybe she might bring me—that's once in a while. If a car's going, she'll bring me, otherwise not in case I have a fit.

It is apparent that the seniors in special education had a particularly restricted social life. They went out with friends and brothers and sisters substantially less often than all other groups, including juniors at their own school. They relied heavily on their parents and had to struggle particularly hard to achieve a limited measure of independence. The disabled seniors in integrated education were in general of higher ability than those who remained at the special school (although a child may not join the integration scheme for medical or emotional reasons, even if suited intellectually), but they were confronted with a wider range of mobility problems: at least four used wheelchairs and a further four other walking aids. Nevertheless they were almost twice as likely to go out with friends and brothers and sisters as were their counterparts at the special school. It was clear that the disabled seniors in integrated education expected to be able to participate in a social life similar to that of their peers, and in many respects this did prove possible.

Activities at home

During the course of discussions about home life, we asked children whether they watched television, read, listened to music, played games or pursued hobbies. Their answers to these questions are shown in Table 22.

Watching television was the most popular of these activities for the children, and over nine in ten indicated that they watched programmes regularly. Disability seemed to make little difference to viewing patterns among the junior aged children: almost every child in both groups watched television. However at secondary school age, more physically disabled than able-bodied adolescents watched television, and this was true whether the disabled pupils attended the special or the integrated comprehensive schools. In some cases it was clear that disabled adolescents watched television regularly because it was difficult for them to pursue more social activities. A 14 year-old boy with spina bifida who used a wheelchair commented

> I'm stuck at home. In the evening when I get home I'm stuck there all night sometimes. Even in the holidays I'm stuck in the house sometimes. I just do revision and probably do a few homeworks that I have got left, and after I've done that I watch television.

Although similar proportions of disabled and non-disabled junior age children watched television, considerable differences were found in the numbers of these pupils who read at home. Among the non-disabled, 14 out of 16 children read books or comics at home whereas, at the special school, only 19 out of 29 said they did so. Nevertheless these two groups were not directly comparable. Only four of the 29 juniors at the special school were certainly not neurologically impaired: of the remainder, 14 were definitely neurologically impaired; and eleven were possibly so impaired. This means that some of the juniors at the special school were likely to have limited powers of concentration and, relative to their able-bodied peers, might show a discrepancy between their verbal and reading ability. This may well have influenced their relative interest in reading at home.

At secondary school level, nearly all the able-bodied pupils said they read books, comics or magazines at home. Somewhat fewer of the physically disabled seniors at the comprehensive schools were interested in reading at home and, in special education, only just over half the seniors spent time at home reading (even fewer than the juniors at their school). Variations in the extent of neurological impairment may again account for part of this difference: more than twice the proportion of seniors at the special school than seniors participating in the integration scheme were definitely or possibly so impaired. However, given the small numbers involved, no firm conclusions can be drawn.

Turning next to the children's enjoyment of music, and referring again to Table 22, it can be seen that, at the junior level, listening to music (nearly always pop music) was popular among three-quarters of the able-bodied pupils and among slightly fewer of those in special education. At the comprehensive schools only just over two-thirds of the able-bodied adolescents expressed an interest in listening to

Characteristics of group	Television				Reading				Music				Games				Hobbies				Total
	Mentioned		Not mentioned		Mentioned		Not mentioned		Mentioned		Not mentioned		Mentioned		Not mentioned		Mentioned		Not mentioned		
	No.	% of group	No.	% of group	No.	% of group	No.	% of group	No.	% of group	No.	% of group	No.	% of group	No.	% of group	No.	% of Group	No.	% of group	No.
Able-bodied																					
Juniors	15	93.8	1	6.3	14	87.5	2	12.5	12	75.0	4	25.0	6	37.5	10	62.5	8	50.0	8	50.0	16
Seniors	10	76.9	3	23.1	11	84.6	2	15.4	9	69.2	4	30.8	6	46.2	7	53.8	7	53.8	6	46.2	13
Physically disabled																					
Juniors in special education	28	96.6	1	3.4	19	65.5	10	34.5	19	65.5	10	34.5	15	51.7	14	48.3	8	27.6	21	72.4	29
Seniors in special education	15	88.2	2	11.8	10	58.8	7	41.2	14	82.4	3	17.6	4	23.5	13	76.5	9	52.9	8	47.1	17
Seniors in integrated education	12	92.3	1	7.7	9	69.2	4	30.8	13	100	0	—	3	23.1	10	76.9	10	76.9	3	23.1	13
Total	80	91.0	8	9.1	63	71.6	25	28.4	67	76.1	21	23.9	34	38.6	54	61.4	42	47.7	46	52.3	88

Table 22: Activities at home

95

music in their spare time. This is an unexpectedly low rate for this age group. Nevertheless the comments of an able-bodied 15 year-old girl appeared typical of her age group. She enjoyed

> Playing records...I don't do sewing and knitting and things like that. My sister does, and my Mum, but it doesn't interest me much. I prefer to play records and sit quietly.

Listening to music was a popular pastime with almost all the physically disabled seniors (27 out of 30). This was an activity which they were able to enjoy easily and some of these adolescents were given their own record players. A 15 year-old boy with muscular dystrophy explained

> Now I've got my new stereo unit I play records a lot...Sometimes I think I am luckier than most people.

Games were the least popular of the indoor activities mentioned by the children and young people, although some pupils said they played various card and board games, puzzles and games of make-believe. The latter were particularly popular among the young children.A nine year-old girl with spina bifida at the special school told us that she enjoyed

> Playing doctors and nurses of course. 'Cos I've been in hospital an awful lot. Playing mothers and fathers—all kids' games. I love them. And talking, most of all that's what I like!

Games were more solitary for a boy of similar age with cerebral palsy:

> I play cars sometimes. I go and sit in my Wendy House—I don't do nothing, I just sit.

Overall just over half the juniors at the special school and over a third of those at the comparison primary school mentioned playing games of different kinds in their out-of-school hours. Among the secondary school pupils, however, less than a quarter of the physically disabled and just under half the able-bodied group mentioned playing games. In this age group, chess, Monopoly and various card games were most likely to be mentioned.

Finally we asked the children about their hobbies. Half the able-bodied juniors had a favourite occupation which they enjoyed in their spare time: creative activities such as woodwork, drawing, pottery, model-making and dancing formed the major pursuits, followed by collecting stamps, coins, key-rings and badges. Several children also mentioned caring for pets. By comparison, only just over a quarter of the physically disabled juniors mentioned a hobby and the range of activities they listed was rather more limited: writing and drawing, collecting cars, gardening and making paper hats. Hobbies were less likely than the other leisure activities discussed to be pursued by the physically disabled juniors.

Slightly more able-bodied seniors than juniors mentioned hobbies. However, as might be expected, the type of activity undertaken changed somewhat with age and, for the older pupils, 'going to parties' figured alongside stamp and coin collecting, and making radios, models and paper kites. Several of the adolescents noted the encouragement they received from members of their families. A 13 year-old boy enthused:

I really like making kites, you know, paper kites. My grand-dad makes kites.
I got the idea off him.

More than three-quarters of the disabled seniors at the comprehensive schools mentioned at least one hobby. The range was quite
extensive and included drama, writing, typing, making models, clocks
and jewellery, and sewing and cooking. A 15 year-old girl with
cerebral palsy described her various interests:

I cook quite a lot. Watch television quite a bit. My Mum hates me—I'm
always in the kitchen, always in the kitchen 'messing things up' as she puts
it. Or go up into my room and listen to the radio or records. That's about it
really.

A girl of the same age who suffered from spina bifida with
hydrocephalus pursued her hobbies with a clear purpose:

Typing—I want to get a job with typing in it...Going for walks, because
everyone says 'you're getting too fat'.

To put these observations in perspective, we looked lastly at the
home-based activities of pupils in relation to their social activities as
reported earlier. In Table 23 the eight types of occupation we asked
about are ranked in terms of popularity for each of the five groups
divided by age, disability and schooling. Overall more children
watched television than participated in any of the other activities,
although listening to music and reading were almost as popular. Least
commonly mentioned by pupils were going to church or a religious
meeting, and playing games at home. Most of the groups tended to be
more likely to report home-based than social activities. However it
was notable that the disabled were less likely than others to mention
an interest in sport but likely to place a greater relative importance on
clubs.

Activity	Juniors— able-bodied	Juniors— physically disabled in special education	Seniors— able-bodied	Seniors— physically disabled in ordinary education	Seniors— physically disabled in special education
Television	1	1	3	2	1
Music	3	2=	4	1	2
Reading	2	2=	1=	5	4
Sport	4	6	1=	6=	6
Clubs	6=	7	5=	3=	3
Hobbies	5	8	5=	3=	5
Games	6=	4	7	8	8
Church	8	5	8	6=	7

Table 23: Ranked participation in leisure activities by groups of
able-bodied and physically disabled juniors and seniors
(most frequently mentioned activities ranked 1)

Summary
There was no evidence that disabled pupils were more likely than the able-bodied to come from single-parent homes, nor did it seem that family size was markedly different in the two groups—although more 'only' children had impairments than did not. Children were not systematically asked to indicate how their disabilities had affected other members of their families, but some pupils spontaneously mentioned both positive and negative consequences.

Although disabled children, especially those in special education, were less likely to go out with friends or with brothers and sisters (and friends) than their able-bodied counterparts, they were about equally as likely to go on outings with parents. Indeed the special school pupils stood out in their dependence on parents, and it seemed that such dependence sometimes increased with age.

Many disabled pupils spent much time at home and although they were no more likely than others to say they watched television or listened to music, some pupils indicated that they spent a disproportionate amount of time on these activities because there was little else to do.

About half the able-bodied pupils in each broad age group mentioned a hobby. The comparable proportions amongst the disabled were around a quarter of the juniors in special education, about half the seniors in special education, and just over three-quarters of the comprehensive school pupils. In other words, most of the integrated pupils appeared to have developed interests to fill in their spare time, but only a much smaller proportion of the special school pupils—who had greater needs for leisure activities—had apparently done so.

7 The future

At the end of our conversations we asked the children about their thoughts on the future. Most pupils had things to say about leaving school, where they might live and work, and whether or not they would like to get married and have a family. Some younger children, however, found it hard to think far ahead and were unable to answer the questions.

Leaving school
The first question we put to pupils about the future was whether or not they were looking forward to leaving school. As Table 24 indicates, the physically disabled children were more likely than the rest to say that they were.

Half the able-bodied juniors did not seem to know what they thought, and seven children interpreted the question as referring to the transfer to secondary school. Of the remainder, three-quarters were not looking forward to leaving school. A nine year-old explained

> I like it (at school) 'cos if you're at work you can't just go home—sometimes they say you have to do overtime.

and a girl a year older replied

> Well, if I wanted it tomorrow, I'd have a short life, wouldn't I? Not really, 'cos you know there are so many problems trying to find a job.

Only one in eight of the able-bodied juniors was definitely looking forward to leaving school, as compared with over half of the physically disabled juniors. The latter group could, if they did not join the integration scheme, remain at the special school until they were 16, while the able-bodied juniors would all change schools by the age of 11. None of the disabled juniors, unlike their able-bodied peers, referred to problems they might face on leaving school. An eight year-old boy with spina bifida confidently looked forward to the future:

> Well then I can get a job and do things that I want to do.

The able-bodied seniors at the comprehensive school were almost equally divided between those who were looking forward to leaving school, those who were not, and those who were unsure. A 14 year-old boy from the first group was happily anticipating the challenge he would face:

Characteristics of group	Looking forward to leaving school		Not looking forward to leaving school		Do not know		Total
	No.	% of group	No.	% of group	No.	% of group	No.
Able-bodied							
Juniors	2	12.5	6	37.5	8	50.1	16
Seniors	4	30.8	5	38.5	4	30.8	13
Physically disabled							
Juniors in special education	16	55.2	7	24.1	6	20.7	29
Seniors in special education	8	47.1	4	23.5	5	29.4	17
Seniors in integrated education	7	58.3	3	25.0	2	16.7	12*
Total	37	42.5	25	28.7	25	28.7	87

*One pupil did not answer this question.

Table 24: Attitudes towards leaving school

100

It gives me a chance to prove myself in the world, getting a job and that ... so I don't have to depend on my mother always giving me money.

However two girls, aged 14 and 17 years respectively, viewed such independence with a certain amount of apprehension. They said

I'm not really looking forward to it. Because I don't know what's in the outside world. And because I don't know about jobs and everything. I don't know nothing about that.

and

I'm a bit frightened actually about what to expect because school doesn't prepare you for outside. It sets you work, but when you go outside it's a different thing.

Some of the able-bodied adolescents also recognized that their lives would change socially on leaving school. A 14 year-old boy admitted

I'm not looking forward to leaving school — you leave all your mates.

How did the physically disabled pupils at the same schools view leaving school? As Table 24 indicates, more than half were definitely looking forward to leaving. This is not to imply that they wanted to leave at the earliest opportunity and a 15 year-old girl with spina bifida and hydrocephalus pointed out:

I want to stay on until I can get as many exams as I can. I think the better you leave school, the better job you can get.

Certain provisos were also made by a 14 year-old boy with muscular dystrophy:

After I've learned everything that I can learn, and if I'm confident that I've learned enough to get me a good job. I'm looking forward to it if I know I've got everything that I need to have. I don't look forward to leaving school — leaving it and not having O levels or A levels or whatever I need.

The ambivalent feelings expressed by some of the able-bodied seniors were also shown by the disabled. A 14 year-old girl with arthrogryphosis qualified her reply by saying

I'm not really looking forward to leaving school, but I'd like to leave school some day. Not too quick though!

However a boy of the same age with spina bifida was more emphatic that he wanted to leave as soon as possible:

Oh yeah. Absolutely dying to get out of school. Probably the day I get out of school I'll collapse. Yes, I'm just dying to get out. Freedom.

Both the able-bodied and the disabled seniors at the comprehensive schools mentioned friends they would miss and said they would worry about finding suitable employment when they left school. The future seemed particularly daunting for three disabled seniors and for a larger proportion of the able-bodied seniors. However the pupil who seemed most downcast at the prospect of her schooldays coming to an end was one of the oldest in the sample who explained

As I see it, I won't have anything to look forward to when I leave, so I wouldn't want to leave. But if I get a nice job — or even a place (to live) then I'd say yes. I'd be in fact glad because I've had enough, just about enough that I can cope with. It all depends.

In the earlier discussion of friendship patterns, it was shown how disabled seniors in special education tended to be socially isolated outside school hours. Leaving school may well further restrict the social life of this group, as many will find it extremely difficult to maintain existing friendships and establish new ones. Only two of the 17 seniors interviewed at the special school indicated that they were aware of some of these problems associated with leaving school. These were a 15 year-old boy confined to a wheelchair by spina bifida who commented

> I won't miss all the work or anything. I might miss some people.

and a 15 year-old girl disabled in a road traffic accident who agreed

> I'm not really (looking forward to leaving school)... You'd have to leave your best friends.

Thoughts about employment

For the majority of children (although not for all disabled young people), leaving school means searching for a job. We therefore asked all pupils if they knew what sort of work they would like to do in the future, and although most children gave some answer, their ideas varied considerably. Twelve of the 16 able-bodied juniors could make one or two suggestions but the other four had no ideas. Where responses were forthcoming, however, they were not necessarily realistic and, for boys in particular, the world of work seemed many years away. Of the eight able-bodied boys interviewed, four wanted to be footballers, one wanted to be a fireman, and three were unsure. The eight girls from the same school suggested ten possible occupations between them: nurse (mentioned three times), clerical worker (three mentions), teacher (two mentions) and hairdresser (two mentions). These 'ambitions' were somewhat different to those held by the juniors in special education. First, 11 of the 29 disabled juniors had no idea of what they might do. And second, half of the 20 jobs described by the remaining 18 pupils were hospital-related, as compared with only one in five of those mentioned by the able-bodied group.

Anderson and Spain (1977) have commented on 'an almost obsessive interest in hospitals, doctors and nurses' among spina bifida children. From our study it would seem that physically disabled children in general, and particularly those needing repeated surgery or a single long period in hospital, tend to meet doctors and nurses as well as ward receptionists and physiotherapists, and may begin to identify with medical staff. A nine year-old girl with spina bifida certainly knew that she wanted to become a

> Ward receptionist. There's a ward receptionist in Great Ormond Street. After I'd seen her doing her work I decided 'Susan, here we come' — in my wheelchair I could do it.

Almost all the girls among the disabled juniors wanted to work in hospitals (nine of the 12 jobs described were hospital-related). Among the disabled junior boys, favourite occupations were fireman, bus driver, policeman, footballer and diver. Only one boy wanted to be a doctor. Probably none of the disabled children were likely to be able to do the jobs they described. However as was apparent with the able-bodied children of a similar age, unrealistic choices are often made by youngsters.

Nonetheless choices are modified as children grow older, and all 13 of the able-bodied seniors were able to provide details of a job they would like to do. There seemed to be a greater awareness of different types of occupations and more feasible ambitions were mentioned: no boy wanted to be a footballer! One 15 year-old girl was quite reasonably influenced by a Saturday job that interested her:

> At the moment I work for a veterinary surgeon and I quite enjoy that so I'm thinking of taking it up after school. I wouldn't mind doing that. Not being an actual vet, just being a vet's nurse, helping him... You have to do a lot of training for that. You have to learn about apparatus and things like that... I wouldn't mind doing that.

Three young people mentioned becoming a medical doctor on leaving school, and one of these seemed particularly determined on this.

Nearly one in three of the disabled seniors in the integration scheme had no idea about the kind of work they would like to do. As a 13 year-old with cerebral palsy put it:

> I don't really know what's going to become of me. I really don't know. I've been thinking of what will happen, but I'm not quite sure what kind of work I'll get. Or what I could do. I don't know.

Among the remaining nine pupils in this group, three girls mentioned medical-related occupations. As one of these said

> I would really like to become a doctor. Not just for the sake of saying 'I'm a doctor' but I think that being what people call handicapped, I'll be able to help other people because I know it from their side... I'd love to do that. Also because people have helped me, and I've been able to get along more. I mean I'm able to come to this school now which I never would have been able to do if I hadn't had certain operations. But I would really like to help other people if I could. Like carry on the good work, or whatever they like to call it.

The other two wanted to work in hospitals, although both indicated that they thought it was unlikely that they would be able to achieve their ambition. Of these, a 17 year-old with a blood disorder, who wanted to become a haematologist or a pharmacist, told us

> I want to work in a hospital, and I know that I don't think I ever will because I've missed a lot, and I think I haven't got enough exams and I'm always—I push myself into a position I never want to be in. I want to do exactly what I want to do. I want to be exactly what I want to be, but right now it's impossible. I have to do a clerical job not because people want me to, but because I know if I don't I'll end up on the dole. And it's not what I want to do. I want to work in a hospital. It's my dream to work in a hospital because I've spent so much time there, I want to be living there and helping people the way they've helped me.

Rather similarly, a 13 year-old with cerebral palsy and epilepsy wanted to work in a hospital but thought it more likely she would become a typist than a nurse as

> You've got to go through a lot to be a nurse, haven't you?

It was undoubtedly painful for some of the disabled seniors to accept the limited opportunities that would be open to them— although it should be remembered that able-bodied young people also have to adjust their aspirations to what they can achieve. All the same, there was evidence that some of the integrated disabled pupils were becoming realistic about what they could hope to do in the future, and overall eight of the nine job choices made by this group were sedentary occupations. Two studies (Evans et al, 1974; Beresford and Laurence, 1975) have shown that half of employed adults with spina bifida have office jobs, and it is in such occupations that the physically disabled are most likely to find employment. This was appreciated by a 14 year-old boy with muscular dystrophy who was confined to his wheelchair and who explained

> I'd like to get a job. Something I can sit at a desk and do—nothing like an office job. I'd like to do something to do with art. I like drawings. Draughtsman, maybe. Layout artist, maybe. We've been talking about it quite a bit at school, as we've got options. But it'll come later. The careers officer will come and talk to us.

Finally, what thoughts had the senior pupils at the special school had about their future occupations? Five boys did not know what they would do when they left school, and the remaining 12 described a job of some kind. In strong contrast with the juniors at the same school, none of the seniors (compared with half of the younger group) mentioned hospital-related employment. It is very unlikely that many seniors at this special school will obtain open employment (as opposed to a place at a sheltered workshop or day centre). Indeed, for these seniors the aim on leaving school was not necessarily to gain a full-time job. This was made clear by a 15 year-old boy with spina bifida in a wheelchair who wanted

> To do more for myself, go round on my own... I want to get a car... If I had a car now I could do all sorts of things... be more independent.

Another boy with the same disability, but a year younger, who used crutches found it difficult to envisage his future:

> I wanted to be a pilot, but it just won't work, me having agoraphobia— that's the word. I just can't do it. I would have liked to be a mechanic, but I just don't know anything about cars... with them sticks I doubt if I'll be able to do anything. I'd like to get rid of them. I keep on trying, but I can't.

Five of the special education seniors—i.e. half the proportion of the integrated seniors—mentioned sedentary occupations and the remainder referred to employment as varied as pop singer, electrician's mate, working in a fish and chip shop, and a job with animals. So, in other words, the disabled seniors at the special school had little idea what they would be doing when they left school. Some would have an opportunity to formulate their ideas more clearly during a period of further education.

A place to live

Apart from possible future jobs, we asked the children in our study where they thought they would live after they left school. Table 25 shows the numbers of children who thought they would remain living at home and those who thought they would move elsewhere. Comprehensive school pupils, especially those with physical disabilities, were least likely to think they would stay with their parents.

Just over half the able-bodied juniors anticipated they would stay at home, and a further quarter did not know, and these responses illustrate how most children of this age have not begun to contemplate their independence. Similar responses were made by the disabled juniors at the special school although considerably more (34.5% as compared with 18.8% of the able-bodied juniors) mentioned living elsewhere. The reason for this difference is not evident, but it might be that more disabled than able-bodied juniors know children who live away from home, and that this influenced their responses.

Among the seniors, slightly more able-bodied pupils thought it was likely that they would remain at home than thought they would probably move elsewhere, although almost a third were undecided. A 13 year-old boy summed up the problems as he saw them:

> I will probably stay at home for quite a while until I get a job, say, or win the pools or something. I won't be able to buy myself a house or rent a flat or something, you see.

Interestingly, the position was reversed for the disabled seniors in integrated education, as more wanted, or expected, to live away from home than stay with their parents. A 14 year-old boy with muscular dystrophy in a wheelchair explained his reasons:

> I think I'll live with my parents and then, if I did get enough money, buy my own bungalow and try to convert it gradually into something I could live in—low cupboards, low cookers—everything that I could do myself. I'd like to be independent.

An older pupil emphasized the importance, but also the problems, of independence:

> If I had a place I wouldn't be at home now. But I don't want to leave and make things worse for myself... That's what's delaying me really, you know... The best place for me is home where if anything happens there's always someone to call on... but I'm willing to try. I want to see for myself. If I can't then I'll have to go back home. I'm going to try anyway. It's going to be hard. I know, it's not going to be easy... While I've got the pain in any part of my joints it just goes paralysed... and it's too painful. So when I picture myself in a flat by my own, you know maybe the phone is ringing downstairs and I have to drag myself downstairs. It's going to be difficult, but I can only know by trying.

Living independently and being able to manage without their parents was a potential achievement of particular significance for the disabled seniors.

The seniors in special education presented yet a different picture, as more than half anticipated remaining at home. Nevertheless some of those who preferred the idea of living somewhere else, or those who were undecided, mentioned the advantages that a move could bring. A 15 year-old boy with spina bifida remarked

> I like living at home, but sort of living on your own without your mother and father sort of makes you independent. Me mum was telling me about this

Characteristics of group	Home No.	Home % of group	Elsewhere No.	Elsewhere % of group	Do not know No.	Do not know % of group	Total No.
Able-bodied							
Juniors	9	56.2	3	18.8	4	25.0	16
Seniors	5	38.5	4	30.8	4	30.8	13
Physically disabled							
Juniors in special education	13	44.8	10	34.5	6	20.7	29
Seniors in special education	9	52.9	4	23.5	4	23.5	17
Seniors in integrated education	3	25.0	5	41.7	4	33.3	12*
Total	39	44.8	26	29.9	22	25.3	87

*One pupil did not answer this question.

Table 25: Thoughts on where to live in the future

college. She said you can do whatever you like. You go to discos and you can go to cinemas as well. That sounds good.

For a 14 year-old girl with cerebral palsy and hydrocephalus the attractions of independence were also social. She said

I'd like to move somewhere else and get to know other people, make new friends.

It seemed that the disabled seniors at the special school often needed encouragement before they would consider a move away from home (several mentioned parents making such a suggestion). The more severely disabled adolescents will always need some assistance with their personal care, but this does not mean that they are unable to contemplate a measure of independence provided they feel they will be given support and help when necessary.

Marriage and children

Finally in relation to the future, all subjects were asked whether they would like to marry, whether they thought they would, and if they wanted to have children. The findings are presented in Tables 26 and 27.

Almost half the able-bodied juniors said they would like to get married, a similar proportion were undecided and only two children claimed they wished to remain single. Moreover, five of the seven who favoured marriage thought they would marry. These findings can be compared with those for the physically disabled juniors. Fairly similar proportions wanted to get married in the two groups, but more than twice as many disabled as able-bodied pupils said they did not want to marry. Lastly, fewer of the disabled who wanted to get married seemed confident that they would (57.1% as compared with 71.4%). Numbers are too small to draw any firm conclusions, but it appears that even among the juniors there may be a difference in the expectations of marriage between those with and without physical disabilities: more disabled respondents thought they would not marry and, of those who would like to, more expressed doubts as to whether marriage would be possible. A difference was also found between these groups in the numbers who said they would like to have children: whereas all the able-bodied subjects wished to become parents, just over one in five of those with disabilities said they would not want children. It is not suggested that what pupils anticipated would necessarily happen, but the differences in the expectations of the groups of subjects are nonetheless worthy of note.

Among the able-bodied seniors, it was found that more than three-quarters wanted to marry, only one pupil wishing to stay single and only two retaining an open mind. Furthermore, nine in ten of those who wanted to get married thought they would do so. All those who wanted to get married also wanted children, and none of the seniors categorically stated that they wished to remain childless. When these responses are compared with those given by the disabled seniors in integrated schooling, it emerges that fewer of the latter group wished to marry and more were uncertain what they thought about getting married. And of those who favoured marriage, only half felt this was likely. Moreover, over two-thirds of the disabled, but less than a

Characteristics of group	Would like to marry		Think will marry		Would not like to marry		Do not know if would like to marry		Total
	No.	% of group	No.	% of group	No.	% of group	No.	% of group	No.
Able-bodied									
Juniors	7	43.8	5	31.3	2	12.5	7	43.8	16
Seniors	10	76.9	9	69.2	1	7.7	2	15.4	13
Physically disabled									
Juniors in special education	14	48.3	8	27.6	8	27.5	7	24.1	29
Seniors in special education	11	64.7	5	29.4	3	17.6	3	17.6	17
Seniors in integrated education	4	36.4	2	18.2	–	–	7	63.6	11*
Total	46	53.5	29	33.7	14	16.3	26	30.2	86

*Two pupils did not answer these questions.
Table 26: Thoughts on marriage

Characteristics of group	Want children No.	% of group	Do not want children No.	% of group	Do not know No.	% of group	Total No.
Able-bodied							
Juniors	7	43.8	—	—	9	56.3	16
Seniors	10	76.9	—	—	3	23.1	13
Physically disabled							
Juniors in special education	16	55.2	6	20.7	7	24.1	29
Seniors in special education	8	47.1	5	29.4	4	23.5	17
Seniors in integrated education	5	45.5	—	—	6	54.5	11*
Total	46	53.5	11	12.8	29	33.7	86

*Two pupils did not answer this question.
Table 27: Thoughts on having children

109

quarter of the able-bodied seniors did not know if they would get married. In Table 27 it can also be seen that half as many disabled as able-bodied seniors wanted children and that twice as many were unsure about having children. A 15 year-old girl with spina bifida voiced some of her fears when she said

> I'd like to know what's going to happen if I decide to get married and have kids. I'd like to know how they'll turn out. 'Cos I wouldn't like to see that I have kids that suffer from what I did... I know we can't all be normal, but I'd like to know what causes it.

Several girls wanted to learn more about the medical consequences of pregnancy and the likelihood that they would give birth to a disabled child. A minority of seniors felt strongly that it was their right to be able to enjoy a similar life, including marriage and children, as their able-bodied peers. A 15 year-old girl with cerebral palsy emphasized this:

> Yes, of course I'd like to get married and have children. You should see my sister. She doesn't want to get married, she doesn't want to have kids. I say it's alright then, I'll get married before you. No, I would like to eventually get married. Of course. *Of course.*

To complete the picture, we turn lastly to the views of the disabled seniors in special education. Eleven of the total of 17 wished to marry, but less than half this group were confident that they will do so. A 15 year-old boy with spina bifida confided

> I'd like to get married, yes... You know the friend of mine that has left school and gone to college and I see at the club, well he's got a sister that I talk to and I like her.

Under half the seniors at the special school wanted children compared with over three-quarters of the able-bodied.

The disabled seniors at the comprehensives and the special school demonstrated by their comments that they were aware that their future life was likely to be different, to a greater or a lesser extent, from that of the able-bodied. They realized that they were less likely to marry and establish a family. In some instances, however, it seemed that they were not sure about the effects that their disabilities might have on their family life, and several gave evidence that they would welcome more information on these matters.

Summary
Disabled pupils were more likely than the able-bodied to say they were looking forward to leaving school, although in general they had less definite ideas about the future.

Most of the younger pupils were somewhat unrealistic when asked about the work they might do, but it was particularly noticeable how frequently the disabled girls expressed a preference for hospital-related employment. By senior level pupils tended to have a better idea of the jobs they might hold, and all the able-bodied pupils had apparently realistic expectations. Nonetheless one in three of the disabled pupils in ordinary education still had no idea what work they might do, although the rest mainly anticipated sedentary occupations.

The seniors in special education were fairly evenly divided into those who expected difficulties in finding work, those who mentioned sedentary occupations, and those who seemed quite unrealistic about the future.

Almost half the sample thought they would probably stay living at home upon leaving school, three in ten thought they would move away, and one in four was unsure. It was the comprehensive school pupils, and especially those with physical disabilities, who were least likely to expect definitely to remain at home.

The physically disabled pupils in integrated education were, of all the groups of pupils, least likely to say that they would like to marry and that they thought that they would. Indeed only half the proportion of this group relative to the seniors in special education had expectations of marriage. Disabled seniors in ordinary education were also less likely than other pupils to say they would like to have children.

8 The Picture Tests

Conversations with children about their direct and personal experiences form both the main part of this study and the contents of the earlier chapters. Here, by contrast, we report on the opportunity taken to examine, less directly, attitudes on physical disability and its consequences.

For this purpose six Picture Tests were devised: 'Christmas Post-box', 'Outing to the Park', 'Looking after the Mouse', 'Going on Stage', 'Watching Television' and 'Woodwork Class'. Each of these was based on a hand-drawn picture (reproduced below), verbally described, and a series of questions. The tests were administered in a fixed order (in case some of the younger children did not manage to get to the end of the series) to individual subjects who had been told they would be shown several pictures of a group of pupils at a school for both physically disabled and able-bodied children, and asked a few questions about what was going on in each. It was stressed to the children that there were no right or wrong answers.

These Picture Tests were essentially an extension of the talks we had had with the children, but they gave subjects an opportunity to say what they thought in a more neutral and less personal context, and brought into discussion situations in which there might be interaction between the disabled and non-disabled, but which would not have arisen in earlier conversation. They were also seen as a means, which could be more successful with some children than direct questioning, of gaining insights about attitudes. Despite their potential value, however, the Picture Tests were not intended to provide a rigorous, in a strict scientific sense, examination of attitudes. Rather, as already stated, they were an adjunct to the discussions that had already been conducted with the children in this study.

So, the aim of this part of the investigation was to get an impression of how far, and in what ways, the presence of physical impairment seemed to be significant in everyday school situations. The purpose was not so much to discover the influence of disability when all else was equal, as to investigate its importance in reasonably realistic contexts. Accordingly it was more crucial to present plausible situations in the tests than to confront children with illustrations in which all figures had identical clothing and personal features and all were engaged in precisely the same occupation. Inevitably the variation between figures in the pictures influenced some children's responses—but this simply parallels what happens in everyday life.

Despite such superficial variability, however, there were important criteria common to the pictures. Each, for instance, featured eight school children, all of whom were of the same sex as the subject, and of whom two were white-skinned and physically disabled, two black-skinned and disabled, two white-skinned and able-bodied and two black-skinned and able-bodied. Furthermore each situation was made as neutral as possible so that, apart from differences in race and physical status, it was not apparent that any figure was necessarily better or worse off than any other.

Differences between illustrated figures along the two dimensions of physical status and race were included for distinct reasons. In the case of the former dimension, the obvious purpose was to gain information on attitudes towards physical disability. As regards the latter, there were two main reasons. First, it seemed unreasonable that all the figures should be white as the study was conducted in a multi-racial area and it was felt to be better (in case children's responses were influenced by skin colour) to include equal numbers of black and white disabled and able-bodied figures in the pictures. Second, to put the quantitative findings on disability into some perspective, it seemed useful to compare the apparent influence of disability on choices of figures with the apparent strength of an alternative possible variable. Skin colour appeared very suitable for this purpose.

Most children responded well to the Picture Tests, and all but a few completed the ratings and gave reasons for their choices. The tests were probably least appropriate for a small number of the older and more mature pupils.* The children's responses are presented for each Picture Test separately in the following sections. In each situation orientations towards disability are assessed on a scale from zero to four: one point was gained each time a disabled child was indicated to be one of the two most advantaged figures, and each time an able-bodied child was said to be one of the two most disadvantaged figures. Explanations for choices are classified according to whether they refer to the influence of disability only, 'other' reasons only, or both or neither of these alternatives.

Situation A: The Christmas Post-Box
At the onset of the Picture Tests children were shown a picture of a classroom at Christmas (see Figure 3) and offered the following description:

It is the end of term, just before Christmas, and all the children are gathering excitedly around the Christmas post-box. It is just being opened and all the cards are being handed out.

The aim in this test was to see whether subjects seemed to think that there would be any difference in the amount of Christmas post received by figures with and without physical disabilities. If they did think so, we wished to find out which group would supposedly get more cards, and why this should be. To elicit this information the

*As several pupils did not start or complete the Picture Tests, there are some discrepancies in the number of children indicated in the tables throughout this chapter.

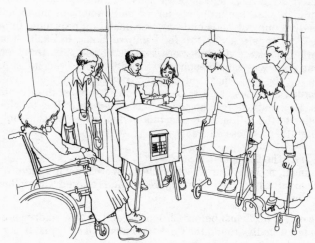

Figure 3: Pictures used in the 'Christmas post-box' situation (*above* version for boys, *below* version for girls)

| Characteristics of group | Disability orientation (Higher scores imply greater tendency to state cards would be received by disabled figures) | | | | | |
	0	1	2	3	4	Total
Able-bodied						
Juniors	2	1	4	2	5	14
Seniors	2	1	1	1	5	10
Physically disabled						
Juniors in special education	3	5	2	5	6	21
Seniors in special eduation	1	1	5	4	0	11
Seniors in integrated education	0	2	1	3	1	7
Total	8	10	13	15	17	63

Table 28: Disability orientations in the 'Christmas Post-box' situation

| Characteristics of group | Reasons given for choices | | | | |
	Disability related only	Other only	Disability related and other	None	Total
Able-bodied					
Juniors	11	3	2	0	16
Seniors	9	4	0	0	13
Physically disabled					
Juniors in special education	10	2	3	7	22
Seniors in special education	1	3	1	6	11
Seniors in integrated education	2	6	2	1	11
Total	33	18	8	14	73

Table 29: Reasons for choices in the 'Christmas Post-box' situation

children were asked a succession of four questions, together with prompts if necessary, for explanations of their choices. The main questions were:

Who do you think will get the most cards?
Who will get the next most?
Who will get the least number of cards?
And who else won't get very many?

Children were required to point to figures in the pictures to indicate their choices.

The main quantitative findings are shown in Tables 28 and 29. Overall, about twice as many subjects were fully consistent in indicating that a disabled figure should receive more cards—i.e. figures with disabilities were selected in response to the first two questions, and figures without disabilities in response to the last two—as consistently cited an able-bodied figure: roughly one in five subjects were entirely inconsistent in orientation, and almost twice this number showed a partial, but not a total, orientation one way or the other. Furthermore, of those who gave reasons for their choices of figures, over two-thirds mentioned the presence of disability while rather less than half described—additionally or alternatively—other influences.

Certain similarities between the groups of subjects emerged. Each of the five, for instance, showed a greater likelihood of pointing to disabled figures as receiving more cards. Nevertheless the strength of this tendency varied and was strongest among able-bodied respondents. Groups also differed in whether or not members tended to give disability-related reasons for their choices—again it was the able-bodied pupils who most often stressed the significance of disability.

One of the most frequent explanations for why disabled figures might gain more cards was that people would feel sorry for them. Reasons given by able-bodied junior school pupils included 'because she's handicapped and gets more friends because people feel sorry for her' and 'one of the handicapped, I should think, because people pity them'. Rather similarly, an able-bodied 12 year-old comprehensive schoolboy said most cards would be received by

> The one in the wheelchair. You know he can't get out of it, he's got to stay in the wheelchair for the rest of his life.

and a girl of the same age at the same school pointed to

> The girl in the wheelchair—because people would feel sorry for her, in a wheelchair all day, and they'll help her and be her friend and send her a Christmas card.

Seven of the 11 disabled comprehensive school pupils completed the ratings, but only four said that being handicapped would make any kind of difference. Of these four, three suggested that the disabled figure would get more cards, and two of these three gave reasons rather reminiscent of those already quoted. A 14 year-old boy, with spina bifida and confined to a wheelchair, thought that people might feel sorry for the disabled figures and say,

> Ah, that poor kid in the chair. He doesn't get much enjoyment. Let's give him more cards than he needs.

The other said

> They'll think of him and they might send him a Christmas card and say 'Happy Christmas. Have a good year, and see you sometime'.

Fewer special school pupils than members of any of the other groups gave reasons for choices made in this Picture Test. However those who did comment also tended to suggest that disabled figures would get most cards because people would feel sorry for them.

Pupils who maintained that able-bodied children would get most cards commonly explained that they would have more friends. As one able-bodied junior school child put it, 'probably the able people' will get most cards 'because they'll be able to meet more friends because they can get out more'. Another pupil presented a similar point of view, although she was apparently not so convinced:

> The girls who're not handicapped know more people. There may be a lot of handicapped people and they might know a few and get on with them and they'd get quite a few cards as well...I suppose all of them get the same, I don't know really.

Comparable comments were made by children from other groups. A 14 year-old non-disabled comprehensive pupil selected a non-disabled figure in response to the first question because 'he's not handicapped and he can go round and mix with people. He's probably got most friends.' And one of the pupil's disabled peers indicated the same. Interestingly, however, only one of the special school pupils suggested that non-disabled figures would have more friends, and indeed two indicated the reverse.

Most, but not all, children who gave disability-related reasons said that disabled figures would be pitied or they would have less friends. A few, however, gave rather different reasons, such as a 14 year-old able-bodied boy who was evidently talking from experience. He commented that the figures receiving the least cards were

> Probably the one in the wheelchair or the one in the kind of things there...Perhaps they keep running into the back of (the other children's) heels with the footplate. With the electric wheelchair it runs over your toes and it hurts.

It was not always easy to follow some of the special school children's meaning—although *they* sometimes seemed quite convinced. Certainly an 11 year-old was most emphatic when she said that 'definitely not them lot, because they're handicapped' would get the most cards. Others, however, were less sure and a 14 year-old girl who had said that disabled figures would both get the most and the least cards admitted that her choices were 'just a wild guess'. Another pupil, having already said 'These four are going to get the most because they're not handicapped', then decided 'I'm confused'.

Although the majority of children seemed to think disability was the most important influence on the receipt of Christmas cards, quite a number of alternative, and equally plausible, interpretations were offered. The junior school pupils thought certain figures might get a lot of cards: 'because he's opening them', 'because the lady's pointing out to her', because 'she's just sitting down, sad', 'because she's pointing to her' and "cos she's got one in her hand'. These children indicated that other figures would, conversely, be unlikely to get many: 'because he looks greedy. He looks anxious for some', 'because his eyes are fixed onto the box', 'because he ain't got none in his hand yet', 'the bully one' and "cos he looks sad'.

Comprehensive school pupils, too, did not always feel that disability was the most crucial factor determining cards received at Christmas. Some stressed that it all depended on how many friends you had, and others maintained 'I don't think I can really tell. It's just a group of eight girls and it doesn't tell you anything about them' or 'I don't know. Probably if they all knew each other they'd all get the same'.

It has already been noted that the integrated physically disabled pupils were rather unlikely to claim that being disabled or not would make any difference to the receipt of Christmas cards. Typically these pupils tended to emphasize personality factors as important, and four specifically said that it was hard to rate the popularity of figures without knowing more about them. According to a 15 year-old girl with cerebral palsy,

> I should imagine it depends on what their personality is (and) who likes them. I don't think there is any significance to the way that this girl's on crutches, this girl's in a wheelchair. She shouldn't get any more because she's in a wheelchair. They should get about the same. As long as people relate to them alright, and they've got the right personality that people like. Of course if someone's very stuck up—'Oh, I don't like you'—she wouldn't get very many.

Other pupils in this group made similar comments implying that sociability was an important factor—figures who attracted comments like 'he seems to be joining in with the others' or 'she's smiling a lot' were thought likely to get a lot of cards.

Situation B: Outing to the Park
In the second test a picture of a group of pupils on a summer outing (Figure 4) was presented to the children who were simultaneously told:

This time it's summer and the children have gone on an outing to the park. They've been having a nature lesson, but now they're having a break and eating ice creams.

Subjects were then, as before, asked four questions relating to figures in the picture:

Who do you think is enjoying him/herself best?
Who do you think is enjoying him/herself second best?
Who is enjoying him/herself least?
Who else might not be enjoying him/herself as much as the others?

Again, respondents were encouraged to explain their choices.

Figure 4: Pictures used in the 'Outing to the Park' situation
(*above* version for boys, *below* version for girls)

Characteristics of group	Disability orientation (Higher scores imply greater tendency to state more enjoyment would be felt by disabled figures)					
	0	1	2	3	4	Total
Able-bodied						
Juniors	3	4	4	0	2	13
Seniors	1	1	3	2	3	10
Physically disabled						
Juniors in special education	1	2	10	6	2	21
Seniors in special education	2	3	3	3	0	11
Seniors in integrated education	1	0	2	2	3	8
Total	8	10	22	13	10	63

Table 30: Disability orientations to the 'Outing to the Park' situation.

Characteristics of group	Reasons given for choices				
	Disability related only	Other only	Disability related and other	None	Total
Able-bodied					
Juniors	5	7	2	2	16
Seniors	6	5	2	0	13
Physically disabled					
Juniors in special education	1	12	3	6	22
Seniors in special education	1	5	2	3	11
Seniors in integrated education	4	3	2	2	11
Total	17	32	11	13	73

Table 31: Reasons for choices in the 'Outing to the Park' situation

Tables 30 and 31 show how subjects responded to the test, both in terms of whether their choices suggested that they thought that disabled or able-bodied figures would be most likely to be enjoying themselves, and according to the types of explanations given for choices. Overall, more than a third of subjects did not seem to think that the presence or absence of disability overwhelmingly affected this enjoyment, and only the minority cited the influence of disability in their verbal accounts.

It is important at this point to note how the situational context affects whether or not disability is a significant variable as shown by the different patterns of responses to Situation B and Situation A. In this second test there was a greater tendency for subjects, overall, to show unbiased orientations towards either disabled or non-disabled figures and, at the same time, a lesser tendency to single out disabled figures as enjoying themselves most.

Contrasting responses to the first and second Picture Tests were also evident between sub-groups. The young able-bodied pupils, for instance, tended to think that non-disabled figures would enjoy the park outing most — although they, as other subjects, had indicated that the disabled would receive the most Christmas post — whereas the older able-bodied pupils tended to think that the disabled figures would be better off, as defined by the tests, in both situations. Nevertheless there was, on the whole, considerably less certainty about distinctions based on disability in the context of the park outing, illustrated, for example, by the fact that half the junior pupils in special education showed no orientation based on disability in relation to Situation B, whereas the same only applied to one in ten pupils in the context of Situation A. Interestingly it was the senior disabled pupils in integrated education who went against this general pattern. They were the only group both to show an increased tendency to stress the greater enjoyment of disabled figures and, in Situation B, to give a majority (albeit a marginal majority) of reasons for choices which took physical impairment into account.

Looking at the comments made by children, it is again interesting to note the many common threads running through them. Generally speaking it seemed that disabled figures were thought likely to be enjoying themselves because going to the park might represent a rare opportunity for them to go out, get fresh air and see somewhere different, whereas the able-bodied might have more fun because they could run about and play. An 11 year-old junior school girl incorporated both these aspects in selecting who she thought would enjoy the park outing most. She chose

> The handicapped ones because they'd get some fresh air...But then I think they'd get a bit unhappy about seeing the others play on the swings and that.

Often, in fact, children seemed to find it hard to weigh up the pros and cons of these two factors, and subjects were divided as to where they placed the emphasis. According to one disabled pupil

> Well it comes down to the person. It depends how much they appreciate things. Quite possibly they (disabled figures) would find it more interesting if anything. Usually when you're handicapped you spend most of the time inside. Maybe to the normal kids it would be like just even going for a walk down the road. It's just an everyday thing. But if someone's handicapped it makes a change to do it.

This point was expanded upon by another physically disabled child who said

> When you've got a bad leg or something and you are in a wheelchair, and when they take you out somewhere—to the park—you just forget about it and just be messing around and you'll be happy, not feeling that you've got a bad leg.

It is not worth quoting extensively from children on their disability-related reasons for enjoyment of the park outing as all comments were very much along the lines of those already described. However it is most important to put these disability-related reasons in context by illustrating some of the other kinds of responses the children made to the pictures.

Somewhat unexpectedly, although as a direct reflection of details in the pictures, a considerable number of children brought ice cream into their discussion. Indeed of the 16 able-bodied junior children, six mentioned the influence of disability upon enjoyment and five mentioned the effect of ice cream, and of the 33 special school children, only seven explicitly mentioned disability in their comments, whereas 12 referred to ice cream. Generally the figures most obviously eating their ice cream were felt to be happiest—as one physically disabled girl put it, 'we all enjoy ourselves when we eat ice creams'—and those who seemed to have finished theirs (we emphasized that *all* children had been given an ice cream) were least contented. In only one case was any relationship established between disability and ice cream, and this was by an 11 year-old girl attending the special school who, when asked who was enjoying the park outing most, replied

> Well definitely *not* that one, because she's definitely not going to get enough ice cream because she's only handicapped and she can't hold anything.

Other children attempted to gauge enjoyment from the expressions on the faces of figures, and whether they appeared interested or bored. Several thought that figures engaged in conversation would be happiest, and those who seemed to be on their own least happy. Beyond these more typical responses, there were also a few rather idiosyncratic observations. For instance one kneeling figure was thought unlikely to be enjoying himself because he might be spoiling his trousers.

Looking simultaneously at figures selected and accompanying comments does underline that orientations, as assessed by a subject's pattern of responses to a situation, and reasons for choices, are not always as much in line as might be expected. Although interpretations can be only tentative, there were certainly some children who responded consistently to figures with and without disabilities when making selections but who made no mention of disability when explaining these choices; conversely there were others who presented inconsistent orientations but indicated that they had taken disability into account. The latter situation, however, is fairly readily explained in that, as shown in Table 31, quite a few subjects did not restrict their comments exclusively to either physical impairment or other influences.

Figure 5: Pictures used in the 'Looking after the Mouse' situation
(*above* version for boys, *below* version for girls)

Situation C: Looking after the Mouse
In this test the picture (see Figure 5) was shown to the subjects with the following description:

Again it's the end of term. All the children are gathered around the school mouse. As there's going to be nobody at the school during the holidays, someone has to take the mouse home and look after it. Everybody wants to take the mouse home, but the children have to choose among themselves who is able to.

The questions that followed this time were:

Who do you think they choose first?
And who do you think they choose next?
Who is the least likely to be chosen?
And who else is less likely than the others to be chosen?

Analysis of children's responses (see Tables 32 and 33) indicates that over three-quarters of subjects were biased towards the selection of either disabled or non-disabled figures, although less than half of these were completely consistently biased. Moreover of this latter group just under half indicated that able-bodied figures would more likely be given the responsibility for looking after the mouse, whereas just over half seemed to think that the reverse was more probable. However there were differences between the groups of pupils in that the strongest tendency to suggest that the safekeeping of the mouse should fall to non-disabled figures was shown by able-bodied juniors, and seniors in special education, whereas this responsibility was most often given to physically disabled figures by able-bodied seniors and disabled juniors in special education. No tendency one way or the other was noted for the small group of integrated disabled pupils for whom these tests were suitable.

Types of reasons given by pupils for choices also varied. Overall there was very little difference in the numbers mentioning disability-related, and other, reasons although it is interesting to note that more gave both kinds of explanation than had done in either of the two tests already described. Generally speaking the able-bodied seniors were most likely to mention the influence of disability, juniors in special education and disabled seniors in the integrated provision were most likely to cite other influences, and both younger pupils in the ordinary junior school and older pupils in special education showed no particular tendency to give one of these types of response rather than the other.

As in the other Picture Tests, where children did give reasons for choices of figures these tended to fall into distinct categories. If disabled figures were explicitly favoured for looking after the mouse, this was usually to give the disabled children something to do. A ten year-old at the ordinary junior school made this point when she selected

The girl in the handicap thing because she wouldn't be able to get out without anyone else and it would give her enjoyment.

Much the same observation was made by an older, also able-bodied, pupil:

Characteristics of group	Disability orientation (Higher scores imply greater tendency to state that mouse would be looked after by disabled figures)					
	0	1	2	3	4	Total
Able-bodied						
Juniors	2	5	3	1	2	13
Seniors	2	3	0	1	4	10
Physically disabled						
Juniors in special education	3	6	3	4	5	21
Seniors in special education	2	2	5	2	0	11
Seniors in integrated education	1	1	3	1	1	7
Total	10	17	14	9	12	62

Table 32: Disability orientations in the 'Looking after the Mouse' situation.

Characteristics of group	Reasons given for choices				
	Disability related only	Other only	Disability related and other	None	Total
Able-bodied					
Juniors	6	4	3	3	16
Seniors	7	2	3	1	13
Physically disabled					
Juniors in special education	3	8	5	6	22
Seniors in special education	2	2	3	4	11
Seniors in integrated education	3	7	1	0	11
Total	21	23	15	14	73

Table 33: Reasons for choices in the 'Looking after the Mouse' situation

I think they might choose one of the handicapped children because it would give her some responsibility and it would help her to look after it. So, one day, her mum might let her have one — if she thinks she could look after it.

The related reason, which many children also gave, is that the active and physically able figures would be particularly *unlikely* to be given the responsibility of the mouse. This was the viewpoint of one boy who said

Well it might be him (a physically disabled figure) because all these other people who maybe aren't handicapped will tend to go out and play and things like that. But as he can't move around too much, he might tend to devote more time to the mouse.

In like manner another boy thought that the able-bodied would not be chosen 'because they can easily walk out of the school and get a mouse'.

Some of the disabled children themselves gave similar answers. For instance a 13 year-old girl with polio attending a comprehensive school selected a disabled figure in response to the first question and explained

She looks quiet and she'll have the time. You know the normal children won't have no time, most of the time, to look after it. They'll be playing football and that. Probably she'll care and look after it because she doesn't have anything else to do.

However, the situation was not necessarily quite so straightforward, as a 15 year-old with muscular dystrophy pointed out:

Well, the disabled children might have more time for it, but...it would depend on what type of thing they do after school — if they had to do physio at home, and how much time they spent on it. I think maybe someone with a handicap might appreciate it (the mouse) more because it gives them a sense of duty really, and responsibility.

Nevertheless, whatever they felt about providing things for disabled children to do in their spare time, many pupils considered the questions raised by this Picture Test in a very practical manner. Many of the able-bodied juniors, in particular, were concerned that the disabled figures would not be able to feed and water the mouse, carry it, take it out of its box and so on. As one eight year-old boy explained in relation to a disabled figure:

When he got home he can't treat the mouse very well because he's handicapped. And then he can't touch it or anything because he has to take off these things (calipers), and when he has to put the mouse on the shelf or something, then he won't be able to get back to his things.

Pupils in other groups also mentioned the problems of management that disabled children might have, although several of the disabled, and older, subjects, distinguished *between* types of physical impairment. For example one boy suggested that whereas a figure on crutches was unlikely to be chosen due to difficulties in carrying the mouse, a figure in a wheelchair might well be selected as he could easily put its cage on his lap. Many of the special school children, who in a very personal sense were all aware of the practical implications of various aids and appliances, drew such distinctions.

As already pointed out, disability-related and other reasons for choices were mentioned with about equal frequency. Generally children tended to say that figures taking an interest in the mouse, and demonstrating kindness towards it, would be able to take it home, whereas those that seemed to be scaring, or scared of, it, or who did not like it—and, in one case, where the figure 'might have a cat or something like that'—would not. 'Grumpy' and 'unhappy' figures also seemed to have less chance of selection. In some cases, however, pupils seemed perplexed.

> I don't know whether they like animals. These are difficult questions to answer really. It could be anybody.

volunteered one 14 year-old, while a disabled girl one year older pointed out how

> It depends on the parents, and whether they let them or not. And also whether they like the animal. Some people hate hamsters and mice and things like that. I don't think anybody in particular would take it home—nobody specific would *definitely* take it home.

Other children, especially in the youngest groups, mentioned the necessity for parental sanction—and two categorically stated that the teacher should take the mouse home!

As in the other Picture Tests, individual pupils did not give the same kinds of reasons for all their choices and, as can be seen from Table 33, they were more likely than in the two situations already described to give a variety of explanations. Also as in the other situations, children who did show a consistent disability orientation did not necessarily give disability-related explanations, just as those with inconsistent orientations may have explicitly responded to the disability dimension on at least some of the four test questions.

Situation D: Going on Stage

Figure 6 illustrates the picture shown to children in the fourth test. Its accompanying description was:

In this picture the children are just filing into the hall where they are going to watch a conjurer performing tricks. When they have settled down, the conjurer will want somebody to go up on stage to help him. Of course all the children want to go and help, but they have to decide among themselves who will go.

Four questions were then asked:

Who is most likely to be chosen to go on stage?
Who would be the second choice?
Who is least likely to be chosen?
And who else is less likely than the others to be chosen?

As previously, respondents were asked to elaborate upon their choices.

In contrast to the other Picture Tests reported so far, there was—as shown in Table 34—a fairly strong overall orientation towards selecting able-bodied figures in response to the first two questions, and disabled figures in response to the last two. At the same time,

127

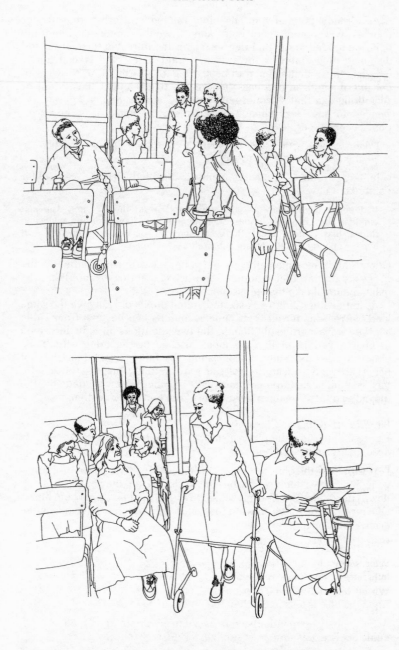

Figure 6: Pictures used in the 'Going on Stage' situation
(*above* version for boys, *below* version for girls).

Disability orientation
(Higher scores imply greater tendency to state going on stage more likely for disabled figures)

Characteristics of group	0	1	2	3	4	Total
Able-bodied						
Juniors	2	3	3	5	0	13
Seniors	4	2	1	1	2	10
Physically disabled						
Juniors in special education	5	2	8	3	3	21
Seniors in special education	1	5	3	2	0	11
Seniors in integrated education	1	2	3	1	0	7
Total	13	14	18	12	5	62

Table 34: Disability orientations in the 'Going on Stage' situation

Characteristics of group	Reasons given for choices				
	Disability related only	Other only	Disability related and other	None	Total
Able-bodied					
Juniors	8	5	0	3	16
Seniors	6	4	2	1	13
Physically disabled					
Juniors in special education	4	5	2	10	21
Seniors in special education	4	2	1	4	11
Seniors in integrated education	6	1	2	2	11
Total	28	17	7	20	72

Table 35: Reasons for choices in the 'Going on Stage' situation

however, more children than in any of the other tests demonstrated a totally inconsistent orientation. There were differences between groups of respondents but these are neither marked nor straight-forward to interpret.

Turning to the reasons given for choices (see Table 35), it is found that fewer children than in previous tests—especially from the junior group in special education—gave explanations. Of those who did, however, more gave disability-related than other reasons, and fewer than in other contexts gave both of these types of reason. The predominance of disability-related over other reasons was most marked amongst the integrated physically disabled group—and, at the other extreme, the juniors in special education gave slightly more other, than disability-related, reasons.

The strong tendency for pupils to suggest that able-bodied figures were more likely to be selected to go on stage reflected very practical considerations. In fact many of the children who brought the presence or absence of disability into their explanations—and most of these within the junior able-bodied and the special education groups—outlined the difficulties of getting wheelchairs onto the stage, especially if stairs had to be negotiated, or of walking there quickly enough with crutches or calipers. A few also mentioned that disabled people might find it more difficult to help with tricks, although some children who mentioned this possibility differentiated between the abilities of children in wheelchairs and those reliant on walking aids. As one respondent put it:

> It depends what the trick is. Of course if it's standing up a lot, people who weren't so mobile wouldn't be able to do it. But there again, if it's sitting down, the girl in the wheelchair could do it. If it was just holding something sitting down, the girl with the walker could do it. It just really depends.

Not all pupils, however, took this line. And three of the eight older able-bodied children who mentioned disability when giving reasons for their choices stressed that disabled figures might well be selected. Of these one said that the main point of the conjurer's visit could have been to make disabled children happy, a second thought the conjurer might feel it would particularly benefit the disabled figures to be involved in the magic and, according to the third,

> It would probably give one of these people's morale a great boost if they were called up by the conjurer—especially if they were the type who thought they were always being rejected and nobody liked them.

A 13 year-old girl in the integration scheme corroborated this viewpoint and pointed out that at the special school she had previously attended

> They always take the people like that (with physical handicaps), just for them to have a try, just to give them a chance. Just to see how it's like—to help someone and to see the audience. Most of the time the people in wheelchairs don't hardly do nothing. They don't have activities or anything.

Some children did give other, non disability-related, reasons for choices, but these tended to be comments more than explanations. Some junior able-bodied pupils mentioned that certain children looked happier than others and so would be chosen, and that others were

Figure 7: Pictures used in the 'Watching Television' situation
(*above* version for boys, *below* version for girls)

talking and so would not. Similar reasons were proffered by the older able-bodied subjects, but the only real reason given by a pupil in the integration scheme was, ambiguously, that the figure selected 'looks the type that can handle it'. The special school pupils tended to say that an interest in magic, a wish to help the conjurer and concentration were the kind of factors that influenced whether or not a specific figure would be selected.

Situation E: Watching Television
Subjects were shown the picture reproduced in Figure 7 in the fifth test and told:

As you can see here, all the children are gathered around watching television. As usual, however, not everybody wants to watch the same programme, and they have to agree who will be allowed to choose which channel they watch.

The questions for this test were:

Which one of the group is most likely to be allowed to choose which programme they watch?
Who is next most likely to choose?
Which boy/girl do you think is least likely to be allowed to choose?
Who else is less likely than the others to be able to choose?

and these, as ever, were followed up with prompts for explanations of choices.

How subjects rated the figures in the picture is shown in Table 36. Overall they were more likely to indicate consistently that disabled figures would be permitted more choice than the non-disabled (eight and three children indicated these extremes respectively), although over one in three of the total sample were totally inconsistent in orientation. Indeed it was the able-bodied seniors who showed much the strongest inclination to state that disabled figures would be most privileged in this context, and the ratings of this group contribute substantially to the overall findings. Members of most groups tended to balance each other in orientation, and the seniors in special education actually went against the general trend by according greater choice to non-disabled figures.

Of subjects who mentioned reasons for their choices, less than half as many gave only disability-related as gave only other explanations, a fifth as many again giving both types of interpretation (see Table 37). It was the juniors in special education who were markedly least likely to mention disability in their comments, but it was only the able-bodied seniors who were more likely than not to imply that the presence or absence of a physical impairment would influence being allowed to select viewing programmes.

Most of the children to imply that disability might influence whether a figure could select television programmes for the class, tended to give the same kinds of reasons as had been given in the Christmas Post-box Picture Test. That is, many stressed that fellow pupils might feel sorry for their disabled peers and so let them choose. By way of illustration, a nine year-old able-bodied girl commented

Characteristics of group	Disability orientation (Higher scores imply greater tendency to state that TV programmes will be chosen by disabled figures)					
	0	1	2	3	4	Total
Able-bodied						
Juniors	1	3	4	4	1	13
Seniors	0	1	1	3	5	10
Physically disabled						
Juniors in special education	0	4	12	4	1	21
Seniors in special education	2	4	2	3	0	11
Seniors in integrated education	0	1	3	2	1	7
Total	3	13	22	16	8	62

Table 36: Disability orientations in the 'Watching Television' situation

Characteristics of group	Reasons given for choices				
	Disability related only	Other only	Disability related and other	None	Total
Able-bodied					
Juniors	3	7	2	4	16
Seniors	7	4	1	1	13
Physically disabled					
Juniors in special education	1	10	3	7	21
Seniors in special education	2	4	0	5	11
Seniors in integrated education	0	3	2	4	9
Total	13	28	8	21	70

Table 37: Reasons for choices in the 'Watching Television' situation

> She can't walk and so they feel sorry for her and let her do what she wants.

and a 13 year-old, also able-bodied, said that the channel should be selected by

> The girl in the wheelchair, because some of them can run about and play but she's got to stay in the wheelchair all the time. So they thought it's time that she had a chance too to do what she wanted to do.

One of the children in this group pointed out that many disabled children would have spent so much time learning to walk that they would not have had much opportunity to watch television; consequently they should be allowed to select programmes.

Only two of the integrated physically disabled pupils mentioned disability in their comments relating to this Picture Test, but both these were in line with those quoted above. However only one of the six special school children who thought that disability was a relevant factor suggested that those with physical impairments should be most favoured when it came to choosing which television channel to watch.

All the other children who gave disability-related reasons laid the stress more on physical, than altruistic, considerations. One younger able-bodied pupil pointed out that 'if you're handicapped it's harder to get to the telly and change it', and an older able-bodied pupil made a similar observation. Most such responses, however, came from the special school pupils, four of whom again stressed how disabled figures would not be able to move quickly enough to be able to change channels first. An 11 year-old girl was particularly deprecating of one of the figures and said '. . . she can't manage because she's mentally handicapped'.

As has already been pointed out, fewer pupils gave disability-related than gave other types of responses. Among the explanations given by the ordinary junior school pupils, three mentioned that the oldest figures would be able to choose the television channel, three mentioned that the happier, non-argumentative figures could, and two picked the figures showing the greatest interest. Three of the four older able-bodied subjects who gave 'other' reasons also stressed the significance of interest and concentration, whereas the fourth concluded that the issue would probably be resolved by a vote. Interest was also most often cited as the crucial deciding factor by the integrated disabled children who gave 'other' reasons.

Children attending the special school seemed particularly likely to give non-disability-related reasons as to why one child rather than another should select television programmes. Some of the comments made by this group are hard to classify, but others made points similar to those made by the other groups of children. Thus age, size—'she looks like she'll beat the others up: she looks big and fat and strong'—and interest in watching TV, were the predominant influences mentioned. Two children moreover suggested that a vote should be taken, and one adamantly claimed that 'none of them' should choose, 'because they're supposed to watch the programme what their teacher watches'.

Situation F: Woodwork Class
This was the final Picture Test. It used the pictures shown in Figure 8,

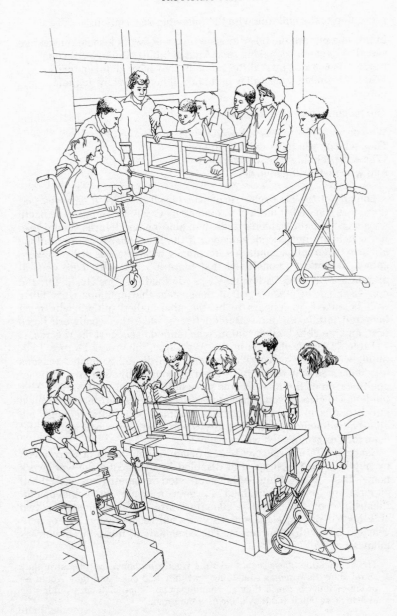

Figure 8: Pictures used in the 'Woodwork Class' situation (*above* version for boys, *below* version for girls)

presented to the children with the following description:

In this last picture the boys/girls are in a woodwork lesson. As you can see, they seem to be making some kind of table. Although only one boy/girl is working on it at the moment, they have all taken turns. When it is finished they all want to take it home to show to their parents.

The respondents were then asked:

Who do you think will be allowed to take it home first?
Then who do you think will take it home?
Who will probably take it home last?
And who just before him/her?

Looking at the children's responses (see Table 38), it emerges that there was somewhat more of a tendency, overall, for pupils to indicate consistently that disabled rather than able-bodied figures should take the woodwork home first. However if the less consistent orientations are also taken into account, i.e. instances where scores of 1 or 3 were gained, it could be concluded that there is marginally more general orientation towards advantage, as defined in this test, for the non-disabled. In other words it does seem that opinions were fairly well balanced: it appears to be the able-bodied juniors who most favoured letting the non-disabled figures take the woodwork home first, and the able-bodied seniors who tended to suggest the reverse.

Table 39 shows that, as in the 'Watching Television' Picture Test, pupils were twice as likely to give only non-disability-related reasons for choices as only disability-related reasons—although an additional one in seven of the total sample gave both types of explanation. This tendency to give reasons unrelated to disability was strongest amongst junior pupils in special education, although it is only amongst the able-bodied senior group that any reverse tendency was noted, and even for this group such was marginal.

Several different reasons taking disability into account were given by pupils. Those in support of disabled figures taking the woodwork home first most often either reflected sympathy or noted an opportunity for the disabled to gain a sense of achievement. Illustrative of the latter explanation are the comments of two able-bodied pupils, eight and 13 years old respectively, and of a 15 year-old boy with spina bifida. The comments of these three were as follows:

The handicapped boys (could take the woodwork home first) because they could show their mums something that they had done and they would be proud of them because they are handicapped. Some of them wouldn't be able to do so much and they'd surprise their mum.

I think they'd let the handicapped children take it home first to show their mothers how they're progressing at school and how they can make things on their own.

It's an achievement. (The handicapped figure could take the woodwork home first) to show his parents that he's actually made something, done something at school.

Characteristics of group	Disability orientation (Higher scores imply greater tendency to state that woodwork will be taken home first by disabled figures)					
	0	1	2	3	4	Total
Able-bodied						
Juniors	3	4	3	2	1	13
Seniors	1	1	2	0	6	10
Physically disabled						
Juniors in special education	4	8	2	3	4	21
Seniors in special education	1	2	3	4	1	11
Seniors in integrated education	0	2	3	0	2	7
Total	9	17	13	9	14	62

Table 38: Disability orientations in the 'Woodwork Class' situation

Characteristics of group	Reasons given for choices				
	Disability related only	Other only	Disability related and other	None	Total
Able-bodied					
Juniors	5	7	2	2	16
Seniors	6	5	0	2	13
Physically disabled					
Juniors in special education	1	8	4	8	21
Seniors in special education	2	5	1	3	11
Seniors in integrated education	1	4	2	2	9
Total	15	29	9	17	70

Table 39: Reasons for choices in the 'Woodwork Class' situation

Apart from very idiosyncratic responses—such as that a figure with crutches would take the table home first as her daddy wanted it for eating on—most comments recognizing the influence of disability focused on practicalities. In the main these considered who could carry the table home best, and most of the younger able-bodied children and special education pupils who took this into account pointed to the difficulties that disabled figures would have. Nevertheless two children again distinguished between types of impairment, both saying that a figure in a wheelchair, but not one on crutches, could manage. Some pupils, by contrast, suggested that disabled figures would be able to take their turn in taking the woodwork home if they got help with transportation from parents and friends.

As in all the situations, however, disability was not the only factor that subjects saw as important in distinguishing between figures most and least advantaged. Amongst the ordinary primary school pupils, for instance, six suggested that the ones who had put most work into, or added the finishing touches to, the table could take it first, and three specifically indicated that those who looked bored would have to wait until last. Two other pupils contrasted happy and sad figures, and in both cases the happier ones gained the greater rewards. Similar comments about the amount of work done and interest shown were made by able-bodied and integrated disabled pupils—although one of the latter group did volunteer, 'It could be anyone, couldn't it?'

Much the same kinds of observations were made by the special school pupils, five maintaining that the hardest workers would take the table home first. However this group also introduced some novel responses, one child pointing out that the advantage should go to a nearby figure who had some string ready(!), and another claiming that a figure who 'looks the kind of boy who had lots of friends, and he could show it to his friends' should have an early turn—although not before a boy in a wheelchair. Nevertheless children sometimes simultaneously made various points, and this particular pupil indicated that another popular figure would wait until last 'because he looks a kind of kind boy who'll let all the other boys have a look at it first before he looks at it'. According to another child a figure was to wait until the end 'because he's not a very good boy' and in yet another instance the last turn went to a girl 'because she was the last one to ask'. One pupil, who clearly found the task somewhat difficult, simply pointed to figures from left to right in the picture as successive questions were asked.

The findings overall

Children's responses—both quantitative and qualitative—to the Picture Tests presented in the previous sections illustrate their perceptions of disability, and its influences, in a variety of contexts. Some differences have emerged between the groups of pupils—but so too have similarities. Overall, therefore, it is unwise to draw stronger conclusions on the effects of age, sex, physical status or schooling than those that have already become apparent.

One of the most striking observations, perhaps, to emerge from this part of the study is the different pattern of responses found for each

Picture Test. This is not really surprising, as quite different considerations were involved, but it is nonetheless noteworthy when notions of stigma, compensation, over-protection and so on are so often advanced in very general terms to explain the disabled person's position in the community. Although the situations presented to subjects in this study represent a tiny selection of possible contexts in which disabled and non-disabled persons might interact, they were able to highlight the contrasts between contexts. For instance pupils indicated that disabled figures were more likely than others to receive more Christmas cards or take the class woodwork home first, but less likely to be invited up on stage by the conjurer. The significance of disability as suggested by children's comments also seemed to depend upon context, and pupils showed a greater tendency to mention the influence of disability when describing who would get most Christmas cards, look after the mouse or go on stage than in the other situations. Many pupils also drew distinctions within contexts, and said that different forms of physical impairment would have different effects. Nevertheless there were common threads running through children's comments. Sympathy and practical considerations were often noted when disability was taken into account, and age, interest and mood were frequently mentioned when it was not.

Apart from examining patterns of responses to the six Picture Tests, it is of interest to look at whether or not individual children revealed similar emphases across situations. In particular it seems worth asking how often they showed extreme orientations (whether favouring disabled or able-bodied figures), and in how many contexts their reasons for choices took disability into account. Finally it is of significance to ascertain how far, for individuals both overall and within the sub-groups, there was an association between extreme orientation and the number of occasions on which disability-related reasons were provided.

Tables 40 and 41 show that, overall, pupils tended to show extreme orientations and mention disability-related reasons in a minority of situations: thus 44 out of the 62 children (71.0 per cent) who completed all the tests consistently indicated advantage for disabled and/or non-disabled figures in, at most, two situations, and 37 out of 70 (52.9 per cent) gave disability-related reasons in no more than two contexts.

Nevertheless some children gave more uniform responses than others, and seven out of 62 (11.3 per cent) showed consistent orientations in five or six situations and 18 out of 62 (29.0 per cent) gave disability-related reasons as often. It was the able-bodied seniors who were far the most likely both to show consistent extreme orientations and to indicate that their responses were influenced by the physical condition of figures.

Finally, Table 42 indicates whether or not children who showed more extreme orientations also more frequently explained their choices in terms of the disability of figures. Excluding subjects who did not complete the ratings for the six tests, correlations were established between the number of times a pupil indicated fully consistent orientations across the six situations, and the number of times, again out of six, he or she gave disability-related interpretations

Characteristics of group	No. of extreme orientations shown across the six Picture Tests							
	0	1	2	3	4	5	6	Total
Able-bodied								
Juniors	2	5	3	1	1	1	0	13
Seniors	2	1	0	1	1	3	2	10
Physically disabled								
Juniors in special education	4	6	5	4	2	0	0	21
Seniors in special education	6	2	2	0	1	0	0	11
Seniors in integrated education	3	2	1	0	0	0	1	7
Total	17	16	11	6	5	4	3	62

Table 40: Extreme orientations to physical status shown by subjects in the Picture Tests.

Characteristics of group	No. of times disability-related reasons given across the six Picture Tests							
	0	1	2	3	4	5	6	Total
Able-bodied								
Juniors	1	6	0	0	5	1	3	16
Seniors	2	0	2	1	1	4	3	13
Physically disabled								
Juniors in special education	6	7	1	2	2	3	0	21
Seniors in special education	3	2	2	3	0	1	0	11
Seniors in integrated education	1	4	0	1	0	2	1	9
Total	13	19	5	7	8	11	7	70

Table 41: Mention of disability-related reasons for choices by subjects in the Picture Tests.

of choices. As can be seen there is a very highly statistically significant correlation between these two aspects of response for the sample as a whole. However, when sub-groups are considered separately, it is only for the juniors in special education that this relationship reached the five per cent level of significance. All other groups, except the seniors in special education, showed correlations of a similar order as for the overall group. Their failure to reach significance is in considerable measure a function of sample size.

So, generally speaking, children who were most consistent in favouring disabled or non-disabled figures in particular situations were also more likely than their peers to indicate that choices had been made on the basis of physical characteristics. Nevertheless the association is by no means perfect and, as pointed out in earlier sections, there were many instances in which there was a clear discrepancy between these two aspects of response.

Disability versus skin-colour orientations
The variable of skin-colour was, as explained earlier, introduced into the Picture Tests both to make the pictures more suitable for use in a multi-racial school, and also to serve as a comparison factor in assessing the influence of disability upon children's choices. Table 43 illustrates, for each of the six tests, and overall, the number of extreme orientations and their directions shown by the sample as a whole.

Characteristics of group	No. of cases	r (Correlation co-efficient)	p (Probability level)
Able-bodied			
Juniors	14	0.51	$0.05 < p < 0.1$
Seniors	10	0.55	$p = 0.1$
Physically disabled			
Juniors in special education	22	0.42	$p = 0.05$
Seniors in special education	11	0.14	$p > 0.1$
Seniors in integrated education	8	0.61	$p > 0.1$
Total	65	0.54	$p < 0.001$

Table 42: Correlations between the frequency of extreme orientations shown by subjects and the number of occasions on which their explanations of choices were disability-related

Picture Test	Extreme orientations to able-bodied and disabled figures			Extreme orientations to black and white skinned figures		
	A-B	D	Total	B	W	Total
'Christmas Post-box'	8	17	25	6	4	10
'Outing to the Park'	8	10	18	2	9	11
'Looking after the Mouse'	10	12	22	4	2	6
'Going on Stage'	13	5	18	9	4	13
'Watching Television'	3	8	11	3	4	7
'Woodwork Class'	9	14	23	9	4	13
All Picture Tests	51	66	117	33	27	60

Table 43: A comparison of extreme orientations of subjects based on physical status and skin colour

It can be seen that only about half as many extreme skin-colour as disability orientations were found among the sample. Moreover consistent skin colour orientations, where shown, did not seem to follow any particular pattern; approximately equal numbers of children seemed to point to black and white figures in the Picture Test situations. There were differences between the tests but these did not seem to be related to the number of extreme orientations found for the disability. dimension. It can be concluded that skin colour had less significance than physical impairment for children in our study.

This finding is no doubt partly an artefact of test method in that it must be remembered that whereas children had been talking about disability prior to the Picture Tests, they had not in any way been alerted to racial questions either before, during or after being shown the pictures. All the same it is important to note that no pupil made a single allusion to skin colour, even to the extent of pointing out a figure as either black or white. This in itself is an important serendipitous finding which somewhat negates the frequent claim that skin colour has an overwhelming significance for most children. The additional observation of a slightly greater orientation towards the favouring of black, rather than white, figures is also important in its own right.

Summary
Six pictures, representing typical school situations but including both able-bodied and disabled figures, were shown to the pupils who were asked to indicate, according to specified criteria, which figures would be most and least advantaged, and if possible to give reasons for their choices.

Most children completed the tests and the majority gave explanations for their ratings. In general the significance of disability within the contexts was recognized, although so too was the relevance of a number of other variables. As might be expected, moreover, the extent to, and manner in which disability might be important was not the same in the different contexts. Furthermore not all children in all age, physical status and schooling groups gave similar responses.

In conclusion it seemed that children did not think that the presence or absence of disability inevitably implied relative advantage or disadvantage and on the whole they made fairly realistic appraisals which took account of emotional, experiential and practical considerations relating to disability as well as the broader influences of volition, interest, personality, mood and circumstances.

Conclusion

Talking to the children left us with four general, but very clear, impressions which to some extent conflict with conventional wisdom.

First of all we found that valuable information on the attitudes, experiences and needs of most physically disabled children can be gained from asking direct questions. Whatever their age, the overwhelming majority of pupils gave no indication that they objected to talking about their disabilities and indeed it certainly seemed that they very often welcomed the opportunity to do so. It was only in the case of one or two children who had very recently acquired disabilities that we sensed any reluctance to talk.

Second, it became very evident that although disabled children would clearly have preferred to have been able-bodied, most were realistic about their condition and were well able to see the funny as well as the serious side. In other words they were not constantly preoccupied by the tragedy of their disability. And just as pupils did not at all times feel sorry for themselves, so they did not wish other people to make too many exceptions for them.

Third, it was strikingly clear—both from children's responses to our questions, and from patterns of abilities and behaviour indicated by teachers—that there is no such thing as the typical disabled child. Not only do pupils differ in the causes, symptoms and prognoses of their disabilities, but they also vary in their experiences, expectations, feelings and in their ability to cope.

And finally, as we talked to the children we increasingly came to realize that the disabled and the non-disabled are not really all that different. Of course children with physical impairments are more likely than others to be impeded in their mobility and to have restricted independence, but in many other respects they do not differ appreciably from their able-bodied peers. Physical status is but a single personal characteristic, and both the discussions and the responses to the Picture Tests showed that disability is by no means always at the forefront of children's minds nor is it consistently of over-riding significance. Age, personality and so on affect how pupils feel and respond, and what matters most depends very much upon the details of time and place.

Besides these general observations, we became aware during our study that changes of emphasis and practice in many areas of daily living could do much both to improve the circumstances of the young disabled and to facilitate their integration within the community. We have divided our conclusions and recommendations in these areas into four main categories—information and counselling, normalization, schooling, and public education—and these are discussed below.

Information and counselling

Many disabled pupils told us they had questions or worries about their physical status that they had never satisfactorily discussed with anyone. Certainly an impression of a lack of openness about disability struck us throughout the study. These children often indicated an ignorance about their own condition, and although this sometimes reflected their age or inability to understand complicated explanations, in other cases it was quite clearly because parents, doctors, teachers and so on had never directly talked to them about such things. Usually it seemed that questions had not been asked, and answers had not been given, although on other occasions it appeared that persistent questioning had got a child nowhere.

There appear to be two distinct areas of need identified by these children. On the one hand, they wanted honest factual information, and on the other they required what might traditionally be termed counselling. Neither of these forms of help is, however, straightforward to administer. As children can be reticent about making demands, it is no use waiting for a child to take the initiative and ask for help, but at the same time information and advice should not routinely be given to a non-receptive pupil. Accordingly it is a question of balance and the recognition of individual needs and requirements on the part of all professionals who come into contact with the young disabled. Not all children want to know the same things at the same time, but all have their moments when a sympathetic ear, a sensitive understanding and a point in the right direction can be of invaluable assistance.

It is not always easy to anticipate just what children might want to know. However, as indicated by our sample, many would like more information on disability. Some pupils said they wished to know why they were handicapped, i.e. what had gone 'wrong', and others wondered what kinds of treatment might be available to them, or if they were likely to change for the better or the worse in the future. Occasionally girls wanted genetic information on whether or not there would be a risk of their producing a disabled child themselves. Of course many such questions can be hard, or even impossible, to answer. However many children did clearly point out that they would like to know whatever it was possible for them to be told.

Apart from details of their impairments, pupils sometimes wanted very practical information on schools they might attend or social activities they might join. Importantly, some—especially older—pupils needed to know about post-school opportunities. We noted, and teachers told us, that a number of pupils (and their parents) were very unrealistic about the future. The schools suggested that more resources should be allocated for the provision of specialized careers advice for disabled pupils, and we strongly support this recommendation.

Besides information, many pupils additionally require some form of counselling, by which we mean someone who will spend time with a child talking and listening, and helping to explore problems which may be worrying or upsetting. It is usual that the person who offers this form of help has been trained in skills which facilitate the expression of feelings, and that this person is not related to the 'client'.

It became clear from speaking to the children that they often did not have the opportunity to talk about themselves and their disabilities with anyone, whether parent, doctor, teacher or social worker. The readiness with which they told us about various aspects of their lives seemed to indicate that for many this was an unfulfilled need. Indeed it has been suggested that there is a certain reluctance among some professionals to talk directly with children, whether disabled or able-bodied. In relation to social work, Stevenson and Parsloe (1978) comment:

. . . the singling out of the children, as a sub-group, within families was rare: on the whole, whilst the children in the family often remained the main focus of concern, most of the interaction took place between social worker and one or both parents.

This observation appears to be equally applicable to doctors, according to the comments made to us by the disabled children.

In addition to the difficulty which some adults have in communicating with any child, there may be particular reasons for reticence with the disabled child. It may be felt that it is best not to distress such a child by emphasizing the uncertainty of the future—in terms of physical prognosis, education or employment—through unwelcome and unnecessary discussion. However, waiting for the child to initiate the conversation can result, and certainly in some cases has resulted, in ill-informed and confused children and young people.

It is indisputable that disabled children and adolescents have special needs for information and counselling (see Scott et al, 1975; Dorner, 1976). However the distinction between information and counselling may not always be clear-cut, and providing facts on sexual development and genetic matters, for example, may best be done by someone who can encourage questions as well as answer them. Because of the personal nature of such enquiries, these discussions should be held with the individual concerned and not simply with their family or other representatives. It is imperative that all disabled young people have the opportunity to talk about these matters with a skilled and sensitive person.

Although a disabled child or young person may often want to talk privately with someone, there are many topics which are suitable for discussion in a group setting. The social worker attached to the special school in our study ran a discussion group, or 'working lunch', for the disabled seniors attending one of the comprehensive schools. This group ran successfully for several years and its members offered each other mutual support when, for example, teasing was encountered. Plans were under way for similar discussion groups for the seniors in special education, and it seems that comparable schemes should be recommended practice in all such schools in all localities.

'Counselling' need not *always* be undertaken by a professional, as often what is chiefly required is someone who will listen to, and take account of, the disabled child's point of view — and this person may be a parent or friend, a teacher or a social worker. In other words, we do not wish to imply that only people with special qualifications or qualities can talk to a disabled child. There are times when specialist skills are required, but there are equally many other times when patience and understanding are the main characteristics needed.

Towards normalization

The fundamental difference between most disabled and most non-disabled children — especially in integrated education — is in their ability, physically, to get around and about. The difficulties faced by the disabled, nonetheless, frequently lead to other kinds of disadvantages. In particular, and as we have seen, disabled pupils tend to lead more restricted social lives than their peers and they are likely to have fewer opportunities for independence and employment when they leave school.

Unfortunately it is rarely possible to eliminate physical disabilities — although good aids and appliances can help to reduce restrictions on mobility. However it is feasible to prevent physical disabilities becoming social handicaps, and this is the principle of normalization which aims not to make *people* normal so much as to make their *conditions* normal.

There are many areas in which the normalization of physically disabled children can be encouraged, but perhaps of foremost importance is in their social life. Many children mentioned the benefits of mixing with 'normal' people and welcomed participation in social activities and outings of most kinds. It is therefore strongly recommended that opportunities for the young disabled to meet and make friends are provided wherever possible. Clubs or trips should, in the main, be integrated, and they should involve young people in activities suitable for their age, interests and abilities. Most importantly, they should also be able to offer transport to participants.

Both pupils and teachers told us that children with limited mobility inevitably rely on more support from others, especially adults, than is usual. Although this is often unavoidable, it is important — not least for the self-esteem of the disabled — to encourage as much independence as possible. Indeed a member of staff at one of the comprehensive schools stressed that integration is not integration if pupils are over-reliant on staff. Most children can do most things for themselves if they are allowed enough time, and it would seem that self-help is often more important than keeping to a rigid schedule.

Being independent is certainly normal, and it is evident that disabled children get a sense of achievement if they can manage on their own — quite apart from the advantages they gain in terms of skill-learning and expanding the range of their activities. In one of the comprehensive schools it seemed that this lesson had been learned the hard way. We were told how practical difficulties faced by disabled children trying to collect several items of food and cutlery in the school dining room, while attempting to maintain their balance or manage aids, had led to the practice of putting all these pupils at one table. The result was resentment and frustration on the part of the children who felt they were no longer being properly integrated.

Of course achieving the optimal balance between providing valuable assistance and encouraging independence can be difficult. This applies to families, teachers, and other professionals. But it is a question on which decisions should not be made lightly, and where account should be taken of practical, social and emotional considerations — including those voiced by the children.

Normalization of the physically disabled should begin in childhood but it must continue into adulthood. In Britain there are schemes to house the handicapped in the centre of the community; cinemas, theatres and other public places have been made much more accessible to wheelchair users, and — for younger adults — there has been a considerable growth in the PHAB (physically handicapped and able-bodied) Club movement. In addition there has been an increasing emphasis on the rights of the disabled to sex and marriage. These changes have, however, been on a small scale. Much more integration is now called for so that encounters between the disabled and the non-disabled can more often occur under everyday conditions. Contact, after all, is the main means of improving social interactions between the disabled and the non-disabled. Better social skills would, additionally, greatly enhance the chances of meeting and making relationships with members of the same and the opposite sex.

Finally, if the future is to have anything to offer the young disabled, there must be good opportunities for occupation or employment after leaving school. For many special education pupils, skills training and sheltered employment may be suitable, but for the rest of these young people, and certainly for the majority of the integrated pupils, it is essential that jobs in the conventional sense are made available. This is particularly crucial in the present economic climate when the disabled are even more disadvantaged than previously.

The vast majority of pupils we spoke to at the comprehensive schools were competent and enthusiastic to work, and it is evident that many of the advantages, in terms of skills and confidence, gained from integration will be lost if opportunities for normalization cease at the age of 18. Many will need sedentary occupations, and a small minority may occasionally require time off for hospital visits, but these young people are determined to prove that they can be useful members of the national workforce. We see it as imperative that disabled young people — and the able-bodied too — do not have their hopes raised during the school years only to see them dashed throughout their adulthood.

Schooling

Just as children differ from one another, so too their schooling needs vary. On the one hand, most of the pupils in special education we spoke to seemed settled and happy at school, and few had any wish to go anywhere else. On the other hand all but one of the integrated pupils with physical disabilities in our study said that, for them, the advantages of ordinary education far outweighed those of special education. Of course children's views are influenced by their personal circumstances and experiences, but it does nonetheless seem valid to conclude that a variety of forms of educational provision for the physically disabled is necessary.

But how should pupils be selected for different educational experiences? The importance of minimizing the risk of a 'wrong' decision means that it is essential—indeed it is required practice— practice—that a range of professionals, as well as parents and pupils themselves where possible, should be consulted. Our impression from the children, and from their teachers, is that young people are suitable for ordinary education if they show a certain determination to work hard at both lessons and social relations, and if they are resilient enough to put up with the teasing and embarrassment they will no doubt encounter. In other words, they must *want* to leave the protected environment of the special school for the challenge of ordinary education. Finally they need to be within the normal range of ability and to be able to cope with the physical arrangements of the school they will attend.

The successful integration of the pupils we spoke to undoubtedly partly reflected the careful preparation that had preceded their transfer. For pupils (both disabled and non-disabled), parents and teachers alike, knowing what to expect before it happens is clearly an ingredient essential to success.

Preparation should take various forms. Children about to be integrated need to know something about their new physical environment, and teachers told us that they often liked to practice moving around the school to see how long it took to get between classrooms. Also they need to get used to the idea of being surrounded by large numbers of active, and often noisy, children who may help, spurn or ignore them. Some preparation for the kinds of lessons they will have, and for the standards of behaviour generally expected, are also required.

Parents need much the same kinds of knowledge to minimize their anxieties for their children and to help them deal with any queries or worries they may have. Moreover, if kept informed about plans, parents can sometimes offer useful information or advice on ways to ease the transition between schools for their child.

Teachers, too, need to be prepared for integration, and in particular for their new responsibilities towards disabled pupils. Many will have limited, if any, experience of physical disability and, as noted by the school staff we interviewed, may feel considerable apprehension. On the one hand they may not be confident about how they should respond to physical problems that might arise, and on the other they can be unsure about how they should treat mixed classes of pupils.

Adequate resources are also essential if integration schemes are to be successful. All the school staff we spoke to emphasized that teachers cannot be expected to undertake additional, and sometimes heavy, responsibilities if they are already under pressure from existing pupils. Resources are likely, in addition, to be needed for building alterations and for new pieces of equipment, as well as for extra transport and other special services required.

Finally, the administrative arrangements of integration schemes should be considered. In the locality in which our study was conducted, integrated pupils retained at least nominal links with the special school they had previously attended. This practice is probably to the advantage of pupils, as it facilitates the provision of welfare staff, transport, medical services and other resources, but it can have its drawbacks. Children are very sensitive to the ways in which they might be labelled, and some integrated pupils we spoke to were evidently resentful of anything that tied them to their old school. This does not mean that links should be severed unnecessarily, but it does suggest that they should be as informal as possible.

Whether children with physical impairments are educated in ordinary or special schools, certain common principles operate. The first of these is that there must be opportunities to mix with non-disabled children. This goal is easily achieved if pupils are fully integrated, and it is relatively straightforward to achieve for partially integrated pupils — such as those in one of the varieties of special unit attached to ordinary schools discussed by Cope and Anderson (1977). Much more effort, however, has to be made to arrange for pupils in special education to meet able-bodied children of their own age through school. Nevertheless, as described earlier, when social activities are arranged between special and ordinary school pupils, they can be highly successful and to the benefit of everybody.

A second principle relating to the schooling of all physically disabled pupils, is that independence and responsibility should be strongly encouraged. Both the importance of social and emotional maturity, and the marked determination of most disabled children to do things for themselves, have been stressed, and teachers in special and ordinary education alike should try to ensure that appropriate skills are learnt and that self-esteem is heightened. This principle extends to the choice of curriculum: the necessity to stretch children to their intellectual limit was brought home to us by the comments made by the pupils integrated into comprehensive schools.

A third consideration facing all teachers, including teachers of the physically disabled, is the differential treatment of individual children. In special education the teacher is likely to be responsible for pupils with markedly different impairments, disabilities and handicaps, and in integrated ordinary education he or she will encounter a mixture of children labelled as disabled and able-bodied. The only possible guideline for teachers is that all children should be treated as fairly as possible. Pupils notice if allowances are made for some but not for others, so that the teacher must make sure that any exceptions made are justified. It is not always kind to let children breach rules just because they have a physical disability: this may not only anger the able-bodied pupils but it may also embarrass and frustrate the disabled.

Much responsibility thus falls on the teacher, who must both exert authority appropriately and set some kind of example for pupils. This role may be particularly difficult for teachers in ordinary education who are likely to have had less experience of disability than teachers in special schools. In our study, pupils in the comprehensive schools tended to suggest that teachers kept a low profile where issues directly to do with disability were concerned. Many able-bodied pupils could not recall any discussion with teachers about disability — although one boy remembered that he had been asked to be helpful to a pupil in his class. In addition, a girl with cerebral palsy said that she thought many teachers themselves were unsure how to treat the children with physical impairments, particularly in the early days of the integration scheme. She felt they took a 'handle carefully, fragile' attitude. Pupils like this girl were especially sensitive to unequal treatment towards children by teachers.

A public education

A recent national opinion survey (Weir, 1981) revealed considerable sympathy for the disabled—despite a certain amount of confusion about what disability and handicap imply, and some doubts about the integration of the disabled into the community. These findings, our own observations, and the literature in general, all emphasize the need for more public education on disability. Their message is summed up in the words of the poster for the International Year of Disabled People:

Do disabled people make you feel uncomfortable? If so, their greatest handicap could be you and your attitude. So, think of the person. Not the disability.

Education on disability should begin at school where there is a captive audience of children at an impressionable age. There was no evidence from our study that the able-bodied consistently regarded the disabled unfavourably, although it did seem that better understanding of, and sympathy towards, problems came with increased age and contact with the physically impaired. Even so, many of the juniors in ordinary education were very receptive to notions of disability, and several expressed considerable interest. Nevertheless in most cases there was a lack of available information on which this interest could be nurtured, and it did seem important that television programmes, films and discussions on disability should exist for youngsters of this age—especially as some might well, later on, attend schools participating in integration schemes.

Older able-bodied pupils were more knowledgeable about disability than their younger peers, and this was probably mainly because they had at least one disabled pupil in their own school class. All the same their knowledge was far from complete and it seemed that disability was little discussed at school. This may be a mistaken impression, but it was one gained from talking to a large number of children. If it is correct, it may be that teachers and pupils alike are embarrassed to raise the topic in the school context.

It is important, if disability is to be regarded as something normal, that issues relating to impairment and handicap are discussed as they arise. It is not suggested that such matters should be raised as a matter of course, and it would be a very bad policy indeed for the disabled to be singled out for special discussion, but it is equally critical that issues of disability are not actively avoided. Such topics might most easily be handled alongside discussion of other groups in classes on social studies.

In brief, there is an important role for schools to play. Optimally they should aim to provide straightforward, basic information on handicapping conditions and to supplement this with discussions on potential problems such as labelling and teasing. Moreover, and most importantly, they should facilitate contacts between the disabled and non-disabled in a variety of contexts. The goal of this entire education programme should be to foster interest in disability, and to make everyone aware of difficulties that can be faced by the disabled and others with whom they might come into contact. Above all it should strive to demonstrate how very different the disabled are from one another and to make sure that preconceptions and stereotyped concepts are diminished.

Schools, however, are but one of a range of influences on children. Families, for instance, have much greater and more prolonged contact with children than do teachers. Partly for this reason, and partly because of their own role in society, adults as well as children need to be educated about disability. Attitudes may be harder to change in later years, but if parents are invited into schools to attend activities in which both disabled and able-bodied pupils are participating, if more naturally-occurring contacts between those with and without impairments and handicaps take place in the community, and if there is a general climate of acceptance towards disability, we may be several steps closer to a well-integrated society.

Finally, mention should be made of the role of the mass media. Television is an important source of information and attitudes and it has a very definite appeal to children: it has been estimated that up to the time of leaving school the average child has spent almost two years watching television. For many adults the appeal is possibly as great, and programmes that treat disability realistically and are informative, but sensitive, can provide an important service for the disabled and non-disabled alike. In much the same way the radio, the national press and a variety of published materials can significantly contribute to the prevailing climate of opinion and knowledge on disability.

Postscript

We hope we have done justice throughout this book to the children we spoke to and to the views they expressed to us. The voices of young people, and the voices of the disabled, too often go unheard, and we are glad to have been able to go some way towards letting school pupils, with and without physical impairments, speak for themselves.

References

ANDERSON, E. M. (1973) *The Disabled Schoolchild. A study of integration in primary schools*, Methuen.

ANDERSON, E. M. and SPAIN, B. (1977) *The Child with Spina Bifida*, Methuen.

BERESFORD, A. and LAURENCE, M. (1975) 'Work and spina bifida', *New Society, 32*, 75-6.

BLYTHE, R.(1979) *The View in Winter. Reflections on old age*, Allen Lane.

BROWN, C. (1954) *My Left Foot*, Secker and Warburg.

BURTON, L. (1975) *The Family Life of Sick Children*, Routledge & Kegan Paul.

CAMPLING, J. (Ed.) (1981) *Images of Ourselves. Women with disabilities talking*, Routledge & Kegan Paul.

CARNEGIE UK TRUST (1964) *Handicapped Children and their Families*, Constable: Dunfermline.

CENTRAL STATISTICAL OFFICE (1981) *Social Trends No. 12, 1982 Edition*, HMSO.

COPE, C. and ANDERSON, E. (1977) *Special Units in Ordinary Schools. An exploratory study of special provision for disabled children*, Studies in Education 6, University of London Institute of Education.

COURT REPORT (REPORT OF THE COMMITTEE ON CHILD HEALTH SERVICES) (1976) *Fit for the Future*, HMSO.

DEACON, J. J. (1974) *Tongue Tied*, National Society for Mentally Handicapped Children.

DEPARTMENT OF EDUCATION AND SCIENCE (1972) *The Health of the School Child*, HMSO.

DORNER, S. (1976) 'Adolescents with spina bifida. How they see their situation', *Archives of Disease in Childhood, 51*, 439-44.

EVANS, K., HICKMAN, V. and CARTER, C. O. 'Handicap and social status of adults with spina bifida cystica', *British Journal of Preventive and Social Medicine, 28*, 85-92.

EXLEY, H. (1981) *What It's Like to be Me*, Exley Publications.

FURNEAUX, B. (1973) *The Special Child*, Penguin Education.

GOFFMAN, E. (1963) *Stigma. Notes on the management of spoiled identity*, Pelican.

GOLDBERG, R. T. (1974) 'Adjustment of children with invisible and visible handicaps: congenital heart disease and facial burns', *Journal of Counselling Psychology, 21*(5), 428-32.

HARRIS, A. (1971) *Handicapped and Impaired in Great Britain*, OPCS, HMSO.

HEWETT, S. (1970) *The Family and the Handicapped Child*, Allen & Unwin.

HILBOURNE, J. (1973) 'On disabling the normal', *British Journal of Social Work, 3*(4), 497-504.

HOLDSWORTH, L. and WHITMORE, K. (1974) 'A study of children with epilepsy attending ordinary schools. 1: Their seizure patterns, progress and behaviour in school', *Developmental Medicine and Child Neurology, 16*, 746-58.

LORING, J. (1975) 'The problem of the multiple-handicapped child' in Loring, J. and Burn, G. (Eds.) *Integration of Handicapped Children in Society*, Routledge & Kegan Paul/Spastics Society.

McMICHAEL, J. (1971) *Handicap: a study of physically handicapped children and their families*, Staples Press.

MORENO, J. L. (1934) *Who Shall Survive?*, Nervous and Mental Diseases Publishing Company: Washington D.C.

RAPIER, J., ADELSON, R., CAREY, R. and CROKE, K. (1973) 'Changes in children's attitudes toward the physically handicapped', *Exceptional Children, 39*(3), 219-23.

RICHARDSON, S. A. (1971) 'Children's values and friendships: a study of physical disability', *Journal of Health and Social Behaviour, 12*(3), 253-8.

RICHARDSON, S. A. (1972) 'People with cerebral palsy talk for themselves', *Developmental Medicine and Child Neurology, 14*, 524-35.

RICHARDSON, S. A. (1976) 'Attitudes and behaviour towards the physically disabled. Birth defects', *Original Article Series, 12*(4), 15-34.

RICHARDSON, S. A., GOODMAN, M., HASTORF, A. H. and DORNBUSCH, S. M. (1961) 'Cultural uniformity in reaction to physical disabilities', *American Sociological Review, 26*(2), 241-7.

ROYAL NATIONAL ORTHOPAEDIC HOSPITAL SCHOOL (1981) *Now This Won't Hurt! An anthology of poetry by children of the RNOHS.*

SCOTT, M., ROBERTS, E. G. G. and TEW, B. (1975) 'Psychosexual problems in adolescent spina bifida patients', *Developmental Medicine and Child Neurology, 17*(35), 158-9.

SIPENSTEIN, G. N. and GOTTLIEB, J. (1977) 'Physical stigma and academic performance as factors affecting children's first impressions of handicapped peers', *American Journal of Mental Deficiency, 81*(5), 455-62.

STEVENSON, O. and PARSLOE, P. (1978) *Social Service Teams: The Practitioner's View*, HMSO.

TINKELMAN, D. G., BRICE, J., TOSHIDA, G. N. and SADLER, J. E. (1976) 'The impact of chronic asthma on the developing child. Observations made in a group setting', *Annals of Allergy, 37*(3), 1974-9.

WARNOCK REPORT (Report of the Committee of Enquiry into the Education of Handicapped Children and Young People) (1978) *Special Educational Needs*, HMSO.

WEIR, S. (1981) 'Our image of the disabled, and how ready we are to help', *New Society, 55*, No. 946, 7-10.

Selected glossary

ARTHROGRYPHOSIS A rare congenital condition, of unknown cause in which the joints are rigid, resulting in the deformity of some or all limbs.

BILATERAL TRIPLEARTHEDESIS An operation to stabilise the ankle joint or certain other joints.

BRITTLE BONE DISEASE In this disease, as its name implies, the bones are very fragile, and multiple fractures occur. Growth may also be affected.

CALIPER A metal support for the leg.

CEREBRAL PALSY This is the name given to a number of chronic non-progressive disorders of the brain which impair motor function. There may also be associated disabilities such as epilepsy or mental retardation. Cerebral palsy has a number of causes.

CONGENITAL Any condition that was present at birth, whether or not it was apparent, at this time and whether or not of genetic cause.

DOWN'S SYNDROME (MONGOLISM) A congenital chromosomal abnormality which is characterized by distinctive physical appearance and mental retardation. In some instances there is also malformation of the heart.

EPILEPSY A disorder of part or parts of the central nervous system associated with episodic alteration of consciousness and of motor or sensory function.

HYDROCEPHALUS This is usually caused by the obstruction, or interference with the absorption of cerebrospinal fluid in the brain. If untreated the skull becomes enlarged: usually the fluid is drained away by a 'shunt' or 'valve'. In some cases mental retardation results.

MUSCULAR DYSTROPHY (Duchenne type) This term covers a group of muscle disorders which are genetically determined and progressive. Although the abnormality is present from birth it only becomes clinically apparent after several years. By the age of 14 most children are confined to a wheelchair.

NEUROLOGICAL IMPAIRMENT Damage to the brain or spinal cord. If the damage is limited it may be difficult to identify by neurological examination. Children who have suffered some neurological impairment may show signs of retarded motor, linguistic and social behaviour.

POLIO This is the colloquial term for poliomyelitis, an infectious disease, which may result in paralysis following damage to the motor nerve cells in the spinal cord.

ROLLATOR A walking aid which is pushed as a support by an individual who is unable to walk without such assistance.

SICKLE CELL ANAEMIA An inherited condition of the blood in which the red blood cells are abnormal. Symptoms include tiredness and pains in the joints or stomach. The disorder is treated by regular blood transfusions.

SPASTICITY Stiffness of the muscles.

SPINA BIFIDA Congenital malformation of the spinal vertebrae, spinal cord and its covering. There may also be assocated disorders of the lower limbs, bladder and bowel, and in some cases there is hydrocephalus. Children with spina bifida often undergo a number of operations.

SPINAL MUSCULAR ATROPHY A progressive disease characterized by weakness, limb deformity and curvature of the spine. Intelligence is not affected.

THALIDOMIDE Congenital limb malformation resulting from damage to the foetus during pregnancy.

Index